The Way of Light & Love

Darlene Franklin Campbell

Copyright © 2023 Darlene Franklin Campbell

All rights reserved.

ISBN: **9798397890205**

All photos and illustrations by Darlene Franklin Campbell unless otherwise noted.

DEDICATION

To Jeanette Petty who took me to meet Love
To Antioch Church, where I first saw the Light.

Photo by Jessi Riggs Taylor

Darlene Franklin-Campbell

CONTENTS

Introduction   7

Chapter 1—Adventure Park
Chapter 2—Jigsaw Puzzles
Chapter 3-Contentment
Chapter 4-I Shall Not Want
Chapter 5-Created for Creation
Chapter 6-Reflect the Mind of Christ
Chapter 7-Forgiveness
Chapter 8-Kindness
Chapter 9-A Merry Heart
Chapter 10- Humility
Chapter 11-Letting Go
Chapter 12-Going Within
Chapter 13-Mind Your Own Business
Chapter 14- Peacemakers
Chapter 15- Cheerful Givers
Chapter 16-Ask
Chapter 17-Stories
Chapter 18-Hope
Chapter 19-The Way of Light
Chapter 20-The Way of Love

I'm so glad you're here, reading these words from the depths of my heart.

When I was thirteen years old my family moved into a rat-invested mill shack, a move I didn't want to make, but it was the great plan for my life. A sweet, mild-mannered neighbor lady named Jeanette invited me to Sunday school and amidst my fears of going to a "church" I went, and to this day I remember the feeling I got the first time I walked in the doors of Antioch Methodist Church in south central Kentucky.

The sunlight poured through the stained-glass windows in that little country church as the choir, led by a small man named Willard, sang, "Oh, how I love Jesus, because he first loved me." The music was sweet and filled with southern twang. The light was warm and welcoming. It seemed alive to me. It seemed like God sent me there at the precise moment to experience it in that precise way.

I felt the love of God, pouring into my soul like the sunlight was pouring through those windows and I knew it was true. There was a God and that God loved—me. It was on that morning that I was being called to walk in a new way, THE Way, the Way of Light and Love.

The first Sunday school lesson I had there was the story of Solomon, who was offered anything he could ever want but all he asked for was wisdom. I went home at thirteen, and sat on the back doorstep of our shack, where I read my lesson, and prayed, "God, I want that, too. I want to be wise beyond my years. I don't ask for wealth. I don't ask for fame. I don't ask for talents or skills. I ask for wisdom. Make me wise." I embraced the teachings of Solomon that day and I embraced the reality and love of God. One year later I knelt as we did in those days at an altar there at Antioch and publicly declared that I decided to spend the rest of my life following The Way.

In the years since then I have gone through many cycles, encountered many doctrines and ideologies, but always, I am drawn back to my first love, The Way of Light and Love. The Way is not a thing. The Way is not a religion nor a doctrine. The Way is an entity, and this entity lives within me and is the life of all I experience. This Way is my existence and my truest friend.

Although I have faltered many times, and erred from my path, The Way is always there when I turn around. Although I may have taken a million steps to get off the path, like Little Red Riding Hood picking flowers in the woods, it only takes one step to get back on the path, even if I've already encountered a big bad wolf or two.

The path is narrow in that it is my path and mine alone. I cannot walk a path that someone else lays out for me, and neither can you. So many people spend a lifetime and never find their paths. I have always returned to The Way and herein lies my life and my love.

I realize that the early followers of the Way were first called Christians at Antioch. How ironic. Antioch, albeit half a world away and 2,000 years apart, was where I first started to walk in The Way.

During the early nineties I became acquainted with the works of C.S. Lewis and found that his words reached across time, befriending me. I connected with him spiritually and that connection has remained. He spoke of The Way as I had not heard it before. I became enamored with his thoughts and teachings.

Speaking of the Tao, "It is Nature. It is the Way, the Road. It is the Way in which the universe goes on, the Way in which things everlastingly emerge, stilly and tranquilly into space and time. It is also the Way in which every man should tread in imitation of that cosmic and supercosmic progression, conforming all activities to that great exemplar." C.S. Lewis, The Abolition of Man, 1947

In 2012, I began learning Bagauzhang and in the process became familiar with a philosophy that Lewis spoke of highly, Taoism. As I read the pages of the Tao Te Ching, like Lewis, I realized that there was no discrepancy between the God I knew, the teachings of Jesus and the teachings of Lao Tzu. If anything, the teachings of Lao Tzu deepened my understanding of Biblical passages, shedding new light on them for me and deepening my love of Jesus Christ, of THE Way.

It has been eleven years since I first encountered the Tao Te Ching but a lifetime since I first encountered The Way. In 2019, I met with a crisis in my life as a pandemic swept the world and life as I knew it was turned upside down, both personally and on a global level. I got lost in all the hustle and bustle and barrage of other people's wishes, thoughts, and feelings. I got off my spiritual path and went flower-picking.

I felt disconnected from the Spirit inside me, so I turned inward for my source of strength, spending quiet moments, whenever possible, reading the Tao Te Ching, reading the Bible, listening to that great teacher, Wayne Dyer, listening to ministers that I respect and communicating with God. This book is a chronicle of my journal entries during this time, my daily devotionals, as I returned to my center and to the Way of Light and Love.

I use several different versions of the Bible, and rely upon Wayne Dyer's book, *Living the Wisdom of the Tao* as it is my favorite version, thus far, of Lao Tzu's classic. I also reference C.S. Lewis, Kenneth Hagin Senior and others as I ponder *The Way of Light and Love*. I hope these thoughts that poured into my heart during this time of self-discovery will bring something good into your life, as well.

And although some of us have never met, you are a part of me, and I am a part of you, and we are a part of the Source of all that is; herein lies the love of God.

Darlene

P.S. I've incorporated a few of my poems, photographs, photos by others and paintings along with my thoughts.

Chapter One
ADVENTURE PARK IN A BOX

When I consider the heavens, the work of your fingers, the moon and the stars, which you have ordained. What is man that you are mindful of him? For you have made him a little lower than the angels, and you have crowned him with glory and honor." Psalm 8:3-9

Once, before there was time, before the earth began or the universe was formed, there was a being made of pure energy.

This energy was the source of all things and the beginning of all things, yet this energy had no beginning of its own, because it **WAS** the beginning.

This being had no name for it knew itself and did not need to be labeled in order to exist. It merely was.

This being had no gender. Gender was not necessary because procreation was not necessary. Procreation was not necessary because all the energy that has ever been or will ever be was already present to produce any manifestation that the being wished for.

The being had no need of physical things like food or water or sleep, because the being was pure energy and though the energy, like light, could manifest in various places all at once, it was still a part of the same source, just as light, no matter where it is found on earth, emminates from the same source. Therefore, this energy was always connected to its source, no matter how far it spread.

Now, since this being was energy, its very nature was to create and it created whatever it imagined. It created simply because it wanted to. So, it decided to create a new realm, sort of like a giant adventure park. The being imaged all sorts of things that could be experienced by visitors, some adversarial, others highly pleasing. All the being had to do to create new things was focus its energy and intention, declare it so and all the components nescessary to produce it came together.

To make it more easily digestible, let's imagine the being as light for a moment and remember that light can be delivered via multiple avenues, lamps, bulbs, windows, etc. And let's imagine the giant adventure park as being inside a big box.

Now, pretend that you're in the box and it has no windows or doors or light fixtures. It would be dark and if you were in there and you couldn't remember having ever not been in there, you might not realize that there was a whole other world outside that box.

Thankfully, the box has peep holes. Every so often a person gets a glimpse of the larger existence outside the box, but it's only a glimpse and those who've never had a glimpse often doubt the words of those who have. They demand explanation but there are no words to explain things that do not exist inside the box because there is no true frame of reference. Some things can't be translated into any of the languages that exists inside the box.

Imagine with me that the box has lots of things going on inside it and for all you know, it's reality. Sometimes, people die and leave their bodies in the box. Those who knew those people mourn them and dig into the box to dispose of their bodies, but you're not really sure what happens when people leave their bodies, only that they do.

Let's say that unbeknownst to you and all the inhabitants of the adventure park, the box is floating in a wide open space that is so vast and filled with lights and colors and objects that you couldn't even imagine because all you can remember is being in the box, which you don't even realize is a box, and you think that is all there is.

Now, back to the eternal being, the initial source all things that exists inside the adventure park, the box. In order to experience the adventure park, the being had to be able to become a part or parts of it, so the being created bodies that could interact with the environment. And just as light can be carried inside multiple vessels, the light or energy of this being was placed inside each of these vessels and whenever two of these vessels got together and followed a certain procedure they could create a new vessel and each time a new vessel was created, energy or light from the source could enter the boxed park and experience a whole new adventure.

However, because the created environment is so realistic and convincing, the vessels developed amnesia and forget what where they originally came from, and in the process, they forgot that they were all connected and that what is done to one is ultimately done to all. The walls of the box, the limits set upon it, they called time and space. The boxed adventure park then continued for generation after generation of great sparks of the originally source taking on the form of temporary vessels with amnesia who go about living in the box as if it is truly reality, only to be ultimately surprised at the end to discover that it was only an adventure, a thrilling vacation of sorts.

Every so often, a light-filled vessel manages to get through life with only partial amnesia. The vessels in the box call them ascended masters. Only one light-filled vessel arrived in this world with complete memory of unity with the Father or Source of All Things.

This being chose a male-gendered vessel and took the earth name, JESUS. This vessel was in complete alignment with Source or Father and this vessel remembered that life in the boxed park is merely a temporary abode and came to remind those who forgot their true identity (to be born again) to remember who they are while they're in the box so that life in the box will be more joyful and abundant. (John 10:10)

This vessel said, "Before Abraham was, I AM." (John 8:58) This vessel said, "I AM the Way (Tao), the truth and the life." (John 1:6) This vessel said, "...he that believeth on me, the works that I do shall he do also; and greater works than these shall he do; because I go unto my Father." John 1:12

I believe we, and all the lifeforms around us, are the vessels inside the boxed adventure park, experiencing a journey into a world of our own making in the sense that we all came from the eternal being made of pure energy. That energy is life and that energy is light and that energy is love and that energy is the Source of everything that has ever been or shall ever be. And the Source of all things inside the park is that being without a beginning or an ending. We ARE a part of that being. I call that being Creator, God, Source, Father and Adoni, El Shaddai, Klonglawiha, Great Spirit, Great Grandfather. I call that being I AM, because there is no true name that is accurate. The being told Moses, " AM, that I AM."

Each day, many times a day, I remember:

You are not your body.

You are not your mind.

You have a mind and you live in a body but you are neither of those things.

You are not your thoughts.

You are not your emotions.

You have thoughts, you feel emotions, but you are not those things.

You are a mighty spiritual being on a journey through a temporay place. You existed before you came into this world as a part of God and you will exist after you leave it as a part of God. So, whatever you do, be mindful of whether it's in alignment with the Way or not in alignment with the Way. All things that are not in alignment with the Way will fade away but those things which are never do.

Chapter Two
Jigsaw Puzzle

When I was a kid, my mom and I spent hours putting together jigsaw puzzles. I got surprisingly good at it. This week I put a puzzle together and as I did, I had a Forrest Gump kind of moment, but instead of thinking that life is like a box of chocolates, I thought, "Life is like a jigsaw puzzle."

WE PUT IT TOGETHER WITHOUT A BOX TO GUIDE US

Except we don't get to look at the picture on the box, because we left it somewhere. And we can't remember where. We are aware that it had an image on it, but we can't remember exactly what it looked like. The nuances escape us. We may have some idea that it was a garden or a yellow cat or whatever, but we don't have the exact image to go by, just some vague memory.

So, we look at the pieces in front of us and try to fit them together. Sometimes, the colors, shapes and patterns match up perfectly and sometimes, they don't. Often, we're like nine-year-old children, trying to cram pieces together that don't really go together and then we get mad because our picture isn't unfolding in a way that makes sense to us.

It's possible to put the puzzle together without the complete picture to guide us. I have done that a time or two. It just takes quite a bit of slowing down the mind and allowing intuition to come into play, paying attention to those subtle variations in colors, sizes, patterns, and shapes of the pieces. I mean you must analyze every piece in relation to the last piece you put down and the surrounding pieces. When we do this, without trying to force the pieces together to create the immediate results that we want, we soon see a true picture unfolding and each time we fit one piece with another that naturally goes with it, we feel a small sense of exhilaration and triumph.

WE HAVE AMNESIA AND LEFT IT SOMEWHERE

We sort of come into this world with spiritual amnesia and the older we get, the longer we go without a view of the "box lid," the less we remember. We start listening to other people tell us how we're supposed to be and what the pictures of our lives are supposed to look like. We start trying to fit the pieces into place according to what others say, but here's the thing. They lost their box lids, too, and most don't even know what their own puzzles are supposed to look like, let alone yours! So, they try to tell you how to put your puzzle together based on what they think theirs are maybe, possibly, supposed to be. It doesn't work. It leads to frustration and to anger.

Some people get so mad that you're not putting your puzzle together like they think it ought to be that they try to force you, even hurt you. Some go so far in their need to control as to destroy another person's puzzle. They may try to control you, trick you, manipulate you, intimidate you, threaten you—all because it unnerves them that they might not actually be the master puzzle solvers they have believed themselves to be. They might get so fearful that somehow it is going to hurt them if they allow you to put your own puzzle together. They might also get afraid someone else is going to damage their puzzles or steal their pieces, so they set up a guard and vehemently guard their puzzles, not allowing anyone in who doesn't follow their prescribed rules for solving puzzles. Others scream at you and tell you how bad you are because your picture isn't looking the way they think it's supposed to look.

Sometimes, we feel horrible about ourselves, and we think that somehow, we're just not good at putting our puzzles together and that there is something wrong with our brains or our hearts or that we are just not "good people." We walk around feeling guilty and unworthy because we aren't putting our puzzles together to please others, or we compared our puzzles to theirs and ours looks smaller or duller or more jumbled. We go to the puzzle "experts," and they tell us how to put our puzzles together. But guess what? They don't have the box lid to our puzzles either!

So, what do we do?

WE CALL THE PUZZLE-MAKER

Imagine that you know that the original creator of your puzzle and that this creator knows exactly where each piece goes. This puzzle-maker comes and whispers in your ear as you put your puzzle together and tells you which piece to pick up and how to turn it and points to the exact place where it goes. There is no stress on you. Your struggle ceases. The only way you can go back to feeling stressed, guilty, fearful, chaotic, etc. is to resist the help being offered to you, if you ignore the puzzle-maker's instructions.

I will interject here that sometimes well-meaning people will come along and point out to you that you are in error, because the instructions you're receiving from the puzzle-maker aren't the same as what they think is right, so they want to remind you that there's something wrong with your hearing and they offer their services to translate for you and tell you that you should follow their instructions as they are clearly more qualified to talk to Puzzle-Maker than you, but they're not, because Puzzle-Maker talks to them about their puzzles and to you about yours.

So, if we trust the puzzle-maker and stop listening to everyone else, we find that we are not only putting our puzzle together almost effortlessly, without relentlessly struggling to jam together pieces that don't belong together, we're also having a wonderful time trusting and getting to know the puzzle-maker.

Each person's life is a unique puzzle that is only finished when we leave our earth bodies. It doesn't matter if anyone else in the world can see that our picture is unfolding as it should or if they can see the complete picture when we're done. It's not their job to see it. It's not even ours. It's simply our job to put our puzzle together and we can either do it without guidance, guessing our way through or we can listen to the soft guiding voice of the puzzle-maker.

"...as many as are led by the Spirit of God, they are the Sons (children) of God." Romans 8:14

TRUST THAT THE PIECES WILL COME TOGETHER

I believe that everything in my life is working out for my good, for my highest benefit, so long as I don't get impatient and try to force the pieces together before the Puzzle-Master tells me where to put them. People can say whatever they want, do whatever they want but as for me, I will follow my internal spiritual guidance system. I paraphrase what King David of Israel once said of his puzzle-maker, "What you say, your word, is a lamp that lights my path." There are times when I don't know exactly what I should wish for or ask for or which way to go, but if I wait, the answer comes. The indwelling I Am in me helps me with this weakness, asking for things so wonderful and deep that my natural mind hasn't caught up just yet and it's not even possible for me to speak or write those deepest desires with ordinary speech. Still, they are there and if I only follow the gentle guidance of my puzzle-maker, the whole picture unfolds, one piece at a time.

So, each of us has our own life path to walk, our own puzzle to complete. The puzzle-maker is constantly whispering to us "This piece goes here," or "no, not there. Not yet." It's up to us to choose whether to listen and trust enough to follow the puzzle-maker's guidance or not. There is never any force involved. If there is force, it's not the puzzle-maker doing the forcing, it's another person without a box lid, another person who can't see the big, eternal picture. If we listen to those Spirit whispers and obey them, our life-puzzles go together so much easier.

As for me, I will live my life trusting the puzzle-maker to guide me in putting every piece into its proper place. If that brings people into my life, great. If that causes some people to walk out it doesn't mean I don't appreciate them, or love them, it just means that my highest call is not to complete their puzzles, it's to complete min

Chapter Three
CONTENTMENT

"The kingdom of God is within you." Luke 17:21

The Apostle Paul once said that he had learned to be content whether he found himself in circumstances of plenty or in circumstances of scarcity. The New Testament was originally written in Greek and the word used here was *autarkhj*, according to Strong's Exhaustive Concordance it meant, *"Sufficient for oneself, strong enough or processing enough to need no aid or support independent of external circumstances contented with one's lot, with one's means, though the slenderest."* And one of the English definitions for content is blissful happiness or a perpetual state of joy. So, what Paul was saying is that he had learned to be happy-independent of the circumstances around him. He had learned a secret. Happiness, true happiness, is not dictated by anything outside us.

IF IT'S NOT out there then where is it?

You may say, "But if he knew what I had to put up with" or if "if he knew what I was going through" he wouldn't be so quick to say that. Here's the thing. Nobody else ever has gone through exactly what you are going through because you are the only you that has faced your unique life with its unique attributes. Each of us have our own path to walk. Nobody can walk it for us.

One thing I realized when my dad died and I was with him as he came to the time to make his transition into pure spirit was that no matter how much handholding I did, no matter how many times I told him that I loved him, when it was all said and done, he had to make that final step by himself. It was his life and his crossing, not mine. We all begin our temporal journeys as individuals, and we all end them as individuals. Yet, somewhere along the way, we begin to think that happiness lies somewhere outside of ourselves. We start to look for someone or something else to "fix" the things that we don't like about our lives.

Some people look for fulfillment in the things they can acquire, in fame, in success, in popularity, in money, in appearance, in social media friends, in relationships and likes and shares. Yet, it's not there and they are left feeling there is something "missing," something "more." And there is, but it's not in the places they're looking. Like that old song says, they are "looking for love in all the wrong places."

THE ONLY PLACE true happiness is found is in alignment with the Almighty Source of the Universe. When you line up with the plan meant especially for you, then you find inner peace, fulfillment, purpose; that is happiness. You realize that you can be happy with or without others and that what really makes you happy is doing what brings you peace in your heart. You have to get in touch with who you are inside, your spirit. And your spirit is connected to the Great Spirit, the Almighty Source of life. You discover that you don't need as much validation, and you're not moved as much by criticism as you once were. Suddenly, you feel you have nothing to prove to anyone, no need to struggle.

WHEN YOU ARE in line with God, you don't need others to perform or behave a certain way. You get that their journeys are different than yours and that your walk is your walk, and you have no need to control them or make them behave the way you want them to. You learn to let God take care of them. You gain peace in your heart that comes from walking your personal God-given path.

If there is a personal struggle involved in the path you are walking, and you constantly feel an internal tug-of-war, there is resistance involved, which means you and God are in disagreement about the way you're going, about the path you're choosing. As long as you have internal resistance, you won't have peace.

"NOBODY GETS ME," I told myself that for years. I looked for a true friend, a real kindred spirit. Finally, I *get it.* It's not anyone else's job to "get me." It's mine. Their job is to get themselves!

Happiness is not "out there" somewhere. Peace is not out there somewhere. It's not dependent upon the right circumstances. My attitude has the power to change my circumstances. Nothing else does. I don't need to wait for the perfect conditions to be the person I'm meant to be.

Just before I started writing my thoughts today, an ad popped up on my Facebook page with a handsome man's face, promising to help me find my "special someone." But guess what? My special someone is the spirit within. No one else can complete me. I'm not half a person. I'm a whole person already.

When you cultivate a relationship with Almighty Source and are spirit-led, you don't need to be with someone else to feel complete. You are happy with others and you're happy alone. If you have an attitude of gratitude every day and refuse to let the fear that the news media and wake up each day, say a prayer of thankfulness, up each day and say a prayer of thankfulness and allow yourself to find joy in your daydreams whether they are logically possible or not, then I promise you, you will begin to see "good" in your world and things will change. One of my favorite Wayne Dyer quotes is, "If you change the way you look at things, the things you look at change."

NO ONE CAN ever see life through anyone else's eyes. If we try to force others to see life through our eyes, we are just wasting our time. We become cynical, judgmental, and bitter. However, we live with gratitude, appreciation, joy, and love, then others will see our light and maybe, they will realize they are light, too, and they will begin to shine.

It's not our job to go around judging another's perception of life. It's our job to live ours. It's not our job to judge. Jesus said that if we judge, we bring judgement on ourselves. Who am I to tell you how to live your life? That's between you and God. Only YOU know what brings peace and alignment in your life. I'm only responsible to travel my own journey.

I finally understand what unconditional love really is. It doesn't mean to look at a horrible condition and love the horrible condition, but it means to walk a life that is in line with God's perfect plan for *you, regardless of circumstances.* That's where happiness is found. That's where peace is at.

Finally, when you decide to listen to the still, small voice within you, to examine your own heart and learn to identify those things that bring you out of alignment with God, out of peace, those things that cause you inner conflict, guilt, confusion, and turmoil. When you learn to withdraw from those things, if necessary, then you are walking in unconditional love because you aren't being guided by religious rules, by someone else's prescription for your life or by the standards of the world's idea of success but you are truly being spirit-led and that is where happiness is found.

STOP TRYING to make things happen, stop the struggle. Stop trying to control other people's wants, feelings and actions so that they produce the end results you dream about. It's not their job to make your dreams come true. Make your requests known to God then feel happy and confident that they are as good as done and listen to your inner guidance system which is the peace of God.

Let inner peace be your navigator through life. If you're having to look over your shoulder all the time, if you have knots in your stomach on a daily basis, if you're constantly sighing and feel a sense of dread, even about things you like, then maybe it's time to examine what you're doing that is throwing your inner peace out of whack.

Chapter Four
I SHALL NOT WANT

Ever desireless.

Desire means, according to the Oxford Languages Dictionary, *"a strong feeling of wanting to have something or wishing for something to happen."* Or if used as a verb it means, *"to strongly wish for or want for something."*

People do a lot of things out of desire or a sense of lack, a sense of something missing. On one hand they may steal, kill, cheat, lie, control, manipulate, and so forth. On the other, they may work hard, strive, try, reach for, set goals, etc. These later things are highly valued in Western society but in the striving, we shut off the important avenue of allowing.

Now, if a person is desiring a thing to happen, that means it hasn't happened yet. If you are desiring a person or a thing that means you don't have that person or thing in the precise present moment.

Not desiring, wanting, feeling need or lack, allows you to really "see." Being ever mindful of a "desire" limits a person to the present version of reality. It hampers the manifestation of Divine provision in that person's life. By doggedly holding on to your own anticipated outcome, you are not open to allowing God's amazing one to surprise you, to bring wonder and serendipity to your life.

You don't have to have it all figured out!

If you go outside to feed your cat and your cat is already there, you don't need to look for him or call him. He's already there. To call for a pet to come in that is standing right in front of you is a strange thing to do. Jesus once told Thomas (I'm paraphrasing here), "You believe because you have seen, but it's those who believe without seeing that are truly fortunate."

Always allowing.

Allow, on the other hand, according to the Oxford Languages Dictionary, means to *"give permission to do something"* to *"give the necessary time or opportunity for."*

Does this mean that you should never act in order to achieve an accomplishment? No. Of course not. I like the way Wayne Dyer sums it all up.

Let the world unfold without always attempting to figure it all out. Let relationships just be, for example, since everything is going to stretch out in Divine order. Don't try so hard to make something work—simply allow. Don't always toil at trying to understand your mate, your children, your parents, your boss, or anyone else, because the Tao is working at all times. When expectations are shattered, practice allowing that to be the way it is. Relax, let go, allow, and recognize that some of your desires are about how you think your world should be, rather than how it is in that moment. Become an astute observer . . . judge less and listen more. Take time to open your mind to the fascinating mystery and uncertainty that we all experience. Practice letting go of always naming and labeling.

Dyer, Wayne W. Change Your Thoughts, Change Your Life (p. 5). Hay House. Kindle Edition.

Or in other words, let go and let God. Make your requests known to God, be grateful that all things are working out perfectly for your life, rejoice and go on about your day. **The joy is in the journey, not in stressing out about the destination.**

The key is in letting go of the wanting, desiring, and needing and sense of lack. There is NO LACK in the Kingdom of God, in the realm of the divine, in glory, in the Spirit Realm.

The Lord is my Shepherd.

I recently looked up every word of the 23rd Psalm in the original Hebrew. Wow, what a powerful message. I simply want to look at the first line of it here.

David wrote,

"The Lord (Jehovah, King of the Universe) is my shepherd (Provider who pastures me) I shall (absolutely, certainly) not want (DESIRE, wish for, lack, need.)

The way of heaven is a realm that you can't see with your natural eyes. You can only see it through spiritual eyes. That is why Jesus told Nicodemus in the book of John, *"...you must be born again."* He said that which is born of flesh is flesh and that which is born of spirit is spirit. You can't see the wind, but you can hear it. You can see the effects of it. *(See John chapter 3 in the New Testament/Covenant)*
Instead of forcing, allow.

Allow inspired thoughts to come to you and then follow them with joy, trusting that all things are working out for you, that God has your back.

Do it without trying to force your own ideas of the perfect outcome. (Proverbs 14:12)

Do it without trying to make it happen on your timetable. (Ecclesiastes 3:11)

Do it without demanding that other people act like you want them to act. Pray for the eyes of their spiritual understanding to be opened (Ephesians 1: 18-19). Leave them to God. Work out your own path to completeness, wholeness (salvation) with respect, awe and wonder at the exceeding greatness of the mighty spiritual force that is able to do exceedingly, abundantly above and beyond anything you could ever have imagined. Stand in awe at the beauty of Heaven's unfolding plan. (Philippians 2:12-13 & Ephesians 3:20)

Do it without constantly trying to analyze and figure out everyone else's issues.

Do it without blaming and shaming.

Do it without a need to prove anything, without ego.

Just allow the Lord to be your shepherd.

"For we are God's handiwork, created in Christ Jesus to do good works, which God prepared in advance for us to do."

Ephesians 2:10

Chapter Five:

Created for Creation

Photo by Brigit Truex, 2022, Berea, Kentucky

"All men will come to him who keeps to the one. They flock to him and receive no harm, for in Him they find peace, security, and happiness.

Music and dining are passing pleasures, yet they cause people to stop. How bland and insipid are the things of this world when one compares them to the eternal Way! When you look for it (the Way), there is nothing to see. When you listen for it, there is nothing to hear. **When you use it, it cannot be exhausted."**
–Lao Tzu

I'm an artist and a writer. When I create a piece of art, it is always first an idea or an image that appears in my mind's eye and ears; from there, it flows out of me to become a creation of some sort.

I take pleasure in my creations as they are natural manifestations of my imagination. So many creations in this world bring pleasure to the five senses, but they only offer pleasure for a little while, unless there is a deep and abiding connection to the ultimate Source of All creation and indeed, it is creation.

I used to wonder what it truly meant to be made in the image of God. In a sense, I think now, that I could say it better by saying we are created in the image of the Ultimate Creator. We were created to create, and this world, this universe, is our art studio, our playground.

DISCONNECTED

When we fixate on obtaining the pleasures of this world because we desire the power and honor they bring, we will still eventually feel empty inside, as if there is something missing. Because we have learned to love the creation more than the Creator. We have become disconnected from the Source of our very own beings.

When this disconnection continues to grow, the lusts (desires to obtain more of whatever it is that brings momentary satisfaction), greed (the unrelenting desire to have control, power, and domination) and the fears that accompany greed tend to grow and grow until the world is filled with confusion and violence.

CONNECTED

However, when we focus on a deep inner relationship *(not adherence to a set of religious rules and theological dogma that condescendingly condemns anyone with a differing viewpoint)* with the ultimate Source of All that is, our infinite Creator, when we seek to be aligned with the Way, we develop a sense of wonder (see <u>Psalms</u> 8) amazement, gratefulness, appreciation, value, joy, fun, harmony, patience and peace.

Our praise, verbal, mental and emotional appreciation, and adoration bring abundance into our lives. This connection to the life-giving Source of All of creation, the realization of WHO and WHAT we really are, is the only thing that can set us free from the illusions and lies that keep us running around trying to obtain what we already have.

Jesus said that those who believed his words and adhered to him were his disciples (followers, students, friends). He said that believing his words and following his words would open his students' understanding to the truth and that the knowledge of this truth would set them free. To be set free is to be rescued, to be rescued means to be saved, but saved from what?

Lies.

Illusions.

Lies and illusions bring bondage.

What lies? How about this one? "You're not _____enough." You can fill in the blank. Or this one, "God won't accept you because_____." Or "You are a mistake." or "You're not deserving." or "You are unworthy." or this one, "You're not acceptable to God, unless you meet these conditions."

And what illusions?

We needed to be rescued from the illusion that this reality is all that there is. Or "You'll be better if...." or "You'll be happy if...." or "You need that person in your life because...."

But Jesus said, "If anyone loves me, he/she will keep my word (follow my teachings). My Father (eternal Source, Abba/All-Providing, ever-loving Papa or Daddy) will love him, and we will come to him and make our home with him." Wow! That's a pretty great promise.

And the words of Jesus were instructions on how to walk in the Way, the inexhaustible divine goodness of the Creator.

There is no lack in the Kingdom of God but the Kingdom of God, the Way, is not the Way of this world. The Eternal Way supersedes finite manifestations of bondage. Therefore, just as artists manifest creations out of the abundance of their ideas, so too, should the pleasures of this life be manifestations out of the abundance of our connection to our creator.

Again, I say, "The Lord *(Jehovah, the Self-Existent Eternal One)* is my shepherd; I shall not want *(lack)*. He maketh *(causes me, permits me, leads me to)* lie down *(rest)* in green pastures *(tender grass, the choiciest homes, places)*: he leadeth *(guides)* me beside the still *(peaceful)* waters." * *Psalms 23:1-2*

all words in parenthesis are taken from Strong's Concordance to clarify ancient morphology in modern terminology.

Darlene Franklin-Campbell

Antioch 1981

September gold shines
On wooden pews, dark
And rich as woodland earth.

I hear Willard singing
Bringing in the Sheaves,
His voice cracking with age,

His black-rimmed glasses, bifocals, sit
On nose's edge, red book in hand
Sleeves rolled up, black shoes shining.

His tenor voice brushes the rafters
As it leaves this world before him
Telling heaven, he is coming soon.

He is coming soon.

*in memory of Willard Page, who shared each light each Sunday as led the choir at Antioch. Willard lived to be 100 years old and made his transition into the realm of glory in 2012.

Chapter Six
Reflect the Mind of Christ

"In your relationship with one another, have the same mindset as Christ Jesus: who, being in the very nature of God, did not consider equality with God something to be used to his own advantage..." Philippians 2:5

In Philippians chapter two the apostle, Paul, lays out how a person can consistently walk in the way.

- Do nothing out of selfish ambition or vain conceit.

If you do things in order to be noticed or praised by others, that's all you get, your fifteen minutes of fame so to speak. The same shallow standards that lift you up one day will tear you down the next. When we follow The

Way, we don't live by those standards. We walk in The Way and those standards are everlasting and enduring.

- Rather, in humility, value others above yourselves, looking our for the best interest of others.

"Heaven and earth are eternal because they don't exist for themselves. The wise puts himself last so ends up first. Serve the needs of others and your own needs will be fulfilled. Let go of ego and the need to be recognized." Tao Te Ching, verse 7.

- Work out your own salvation with reference and respect. For it is God who works in you and to will and to act in order to fulfill his good purpose.

So, instead of being stubborn and insisting on having things your own way or deciding that you need things, circumstances, and people to be a certain way in order for you to be happy, trust God and be content with what you have, knowing that all things work together for your highest good. There is no need to compare yourself to anyone else or to compare your journey to theirs. Your path is your path. Don't look to the right or to the left. Don't worry about what has been or what will be. Just put one foot in front of the other and walk the road in front of you.

- Whatever you do, do it without grumbling and complaining.

King Solomon once said that grievous or bitter words stir up strife, but a soft answer turns away wrath. If you want to see time stand still and stuff fall apart, just start complaining about all that's not right in your life and watch the universe deliver it to you on a tarnished platter.

King Solomon also said that the power of life and death are in the tongue. With the tongue we can bring blessings to our lives, or we can bring curses. The moment you complain, you call those adversarial things that you don't want right into your life.

Complaining, criticizing others, nit-picking and being cantankerous never accomplishes anything good for you. Jesus said to let your yes mean yes and your no mean no and don't make a big deal about it least you draw stuff into your life that you really don't want.

Paul said to speak to each other in psalms, hymns and encouraging words. When you bless others, you receive blessings. When you curse others, you receive curses. When you are thankful for what you have you receive more to be thankful for and when you are dissatisfied and complaining, you receive more to be dissatisfied and complain about. It is a spiritual law that is more solid than the physical law of gravity.

- Rejoice in the Lord always.

Stand in you now moment being pure and positive. The joy of the Lord is your strength. No matter what condition you find yourself in, realize that God's love is unconditional. Find one positive thing, no matter how small seemingly, focus on and dwell on that positive thing, be appreciative of the positive thing and watch the negative thing begin to turn around.

- And again, I say rejoice.

I end this entry by reminding myself of the following:

Don't complain.

Don't compare.

Instead,

Trust.

Lean.

Rejoice.

Chapter Seven
FORGIVENESS

Photo by Rachel A Warmouth

"The world belongs to those who let go." Lao Tzu

PONIES WILL BE PONIES

When I was a child, I had a pony named Lightning. One day I turned my back and he bit me. It hurt. It left prints on my skin. I never forgot how Lightning bit me, but I didn't hold it against him because my mom said, "He's a pony. That's the nature of a pony. Don't turn your back on a pony. Ponies will be ponies."

So, I accepted that biting me in the back was his nature. I didn't hate him for it. I didn't hold onto the pain of the bite. I didn't let it consume me or cause me not to want to look at, talk about or think about ponies ever again. I accepted it and I moved on. All of these years later, I hold no grudges against that pony, nor other ponies who look like Lightning. I am not filled with remorse, regret, anger, guilt, or shame when I remember him. I have let go. I have forgiven my pony. That is an over-simplified example of forgiveness, but the principle is the same. Forgiveness is a law of the Spiritual Universe. Forgiveness is the art of letting go. It has nothing to do with forgetfulness.

LET IT GO

When a human being hurts us, we can either hold onto the pain, the anger, etc. or we can let it go, realize it is the person's nature and get on with our lives. That's forgiveness–just letting go. Holding onto anger toward that person, holding onto pain caused by that person, doesn't punish the person who hurt us. It hurts US (you, me)– over and over and over again. It gives that person power over our lives. It ties us to the past and robs us of joy in the present. It taints our lives. If we hold on to the negative thoughts and feelings, they will drain our life's energy, making us bitter, angry, resentful, and possibly even sick.

Forgiveness doesn't equate to forgetfulness. When someone hurts us, forgiving doesn't mean we don't remember what was done to us or how much it hurt. It simply means we hold no anger or ill-will toward them. It means we acknowledge that they are the way they are, they were the way they were, and we let it go.

YESTERDAY IS OVER

But how do you forgive? How do we let go of the pain? The anger? The years of mistreatment or loneliness or feelings of worthlessness that someone inflicted upon us.

Well, realize that it is the past and the past doesn't have to be our present or our future. Let go of yesterday. We can't change it, can't undo what was done. Think of it like a chapter in the book of life. Turn the page and move to the next chapter. Your story (my story) is not over, so don't stay in a chapter that's already been read. When you feel those old feelings coming back, turn to God and remember that's where peace is found, your connection to the eternal spirit, creator of all things. Realize that you are a spirit, and your spirit is not controlled by anyone or anything that they did to you. You are a great spiritual being and you are greater than anything your body or mind has endured. Get in touch with the source of all things and say "I forgive.... (whoever)" and feel peace flood over you. Forgiveness is a choice.

Realize that it's normal to have anger and hurt and pain. They come when we are mistreated, betrayed, backstabbed, or manipulated, etc., and we are not bad for feeling what we feel. We don't have to blame someone else. We don't have to justify our feelings. We can merely note that we have them and decide how we want to deal with them. But then we have to release them and move forward.

BREAKING OUT OF VICTIMHOOD

Ultimately, if we choose not to forgive, we choose to remain a victim. Somehow, we've had this flawed understanding of an eye for an eye drilled into us. Ghandhi said that if we lived by such a rule then pretty soon the whole world would be blind. Jesus taught to turn the other cheek, which meant LET IT GO! We have to change the way we perceive things. Stephen Covey called it a paradigm shift. Notice I used the word "choose." Yes, forgiveness is a choice. Choose to look at it as a life lesson. The pony bit me. Now I know the nature of a pony is to bite. I don't hate ponies. I realize that a pony is a pony. Stop trying to punish people, guilt people, get even with people, manipulate people, and remember that a pony is a pony. That's the only path to freedom. You can't change people and holding onto anger isn't going to do you or them any good.

There is a Chinese saying, "If you're going to pursue revenge, you'd better dig two graves." In other words, your desire for revenge, your determination to get even, will eventually destroy you. Retaliation is NEVER the answer.

There's a scene in the movie Old Yeller that has stuck with me for years. Travis is sad and regretting the fact that he had to shoot the dog he loved so much. He is having a hard time forgiving himself and letting go of the past. His dad comes home from a long journey and finds him still grieving. He tells him that life is part good and part bad. If we spend all of the good times regretting the bad, then we lose out on the good. In this world people are going to hurt us, physically, emotionally, and mentally. Spouses are going to leave. People are going to cheat you out of money. They're going to sideswipe your vehicle, toilet paper your house, shoot your dog, run over your cats, throw beer cans in your yard, cuss you out on Facebook. They're going to steal from you and lie about you. They're going to throw you under the bus at work, take the promotion right out from under you. And sometimes- they'll do it on purpose. We can either spend our whole lives bitter, resentful, and feeling sorry for ourselves, holding onto the past and the hurt that they caused us, or we can seize the moment and find the beauty that is in front of us right now.

There is freedom in forgiveness.

Darlene Franklin-Campbell

"The heart that is generous and kind most resembles God,"
Robert Burns

Chapter Eight
KINDNESS

"Nothing is so strong as gentleness, nothing so gentle as real strength."
  - Saint Francis de Sales

KIND. NOT NICE. Some people use kind and nice interchangeably but they're not the same thing.

A serial killer can be nice but not kind. Nice is an act we put on to be socially acceptable. Nice is surface but kindness comes from deep within. Nice is born of society, but kindness is born of the spirit.

KINDNESS IS IN ALIGNMENT WITH THE WAY

Like compassion, kindness is not an emotion. It's an act, a choice. It's choosing to help, to be altruistic, even when you know there's nothing in it for you, even when you don't feel like it.

Every day the news is filled with violence, hatred, crime, deception, greed, and fear. These are the symptoms of a society, a world, in the grips of temporal displacement, people believing that this life is all that there is and having no true concept of spiritual universe and its laws, which often lie in direct contradiction to what is trending at the moment or what is popular. These acts testify to people who are spiritually asleep and not in tune with a higher, better way.

Violence breeds more violence and as Ghandhi said, an eye for an eye just makes the whole world blind, blind with fear, blind with anger, blind with hatred. People stop seeing each other as human beings. They say and do horrible things to each other, in the name of politics, in the name of religion–doesn't matter, cruelty is cruelty and if I hate a person, then no matter what I accuse that person of, I am no better. Hatred is a by-product of fear. Violence is never an acceptable way to deal with disappointment or hardship. What was it Jesus said, "If you live by the sword, you die by the sword?" Violence, cruelty, and hatred only lead to more violence, cruelty, and hatred. Violence is never in alignment with the Way and according to both Jesus and the Tao Te Ching, it is direct opposition to the ways of God.

Don't get me wrong, sometimes a person has no choice but to defend himself or herself or the ones they love from violent attacks, but words only hold power over you if you let them. They are never an excuse to be cruel.

KINDNESS EQUALS STRENGTH

When we are kind, we are vulnerable, but the vulnerable are the strongest and the bravest of us all.

To be gentle one must also be kind and have integrity. Gentleness implies that a person has learned to control the savage part of his or herself, the reptile brain as it is called in martial arts or that base part of us that just reacts out of survival instinct and fear. Without gentleness we become no more than educated animals. This gentleness comes from the spirit, but we must choose to put it on like clothing.

What we throw out into the world gets reflected back to us. If I am a negative person, always criticizing others, always offended then I will draw more negativity and criticism into my life. If I have an attitude of gratitude and sow kindness everywhere I go then I will be loved by many, and doors will swing open for me. A kind disposition opens a multitude of doors. *"Kindness is bottomless. Once accessed, there is an infinite supply. Helping others, you help yourself."* Tao Te Ching

"Your own soul is nourished when you are kind; it is destroyed when you are cruel." Proverbs 11:17

If you are cruel, you do yourself more harm than you can imagine. You damage your very soul, your sense of self and become more spiritually blind with each cruel act. Cruelty is poison both to the one it is perpetrated upon and the perpetrator.

Kindness always produces generosity and is a mark of spiritual maturity. Gentleness is the by-product of kindness and goes hand-in-hand with humility, grace, and compassion. Gentleness is a reflection of an inner strength that can only be found in those mature enough and courageous enough to be kind.

Chapter Nine

A Merry Heart

"A merry heart doeth good like a medicine but a broken spirit dries the bones." Proverbs 17:22

I love to laugh. I love to be with people who laugh. Laughter is contagious.

Sure, there are times to be sad, to be angry, and to grieve, but I believe that even in the face of emotional, physical, and psychological trauma, joy and laughter can set us on the road to recovery.

I once read where Moe Howard (The Three Stooges) said that he felt like the only thing he was good at was making people laugh and believed that was his purpose in life. Minnie Pearl (Grand Ole Opry) talked about how she one day came to the conclusion that she would never be a raving beauty or glamour girl, but she had a powerful gift to make a profound difference in the lives of others. She had the gift of making them laugh. Both of these people understood a powerful principle of the Way. There is power in laughter and people need it. Laughter is a gift. Laughter is a healing balm.

The late comedians, George Burns and Bob Hope, who both lived to be over one hundred, believed it, too, that there is amazing power in laughter. According to **Mayo Clinic, laughter can:**

1. ***Stimulate many organs.*** *Laughter enhances your intake of oxygen-rich air, stimulates your heart, lungs, and muscles, and increases the endorphins that are released by your brain.*
2. ***Activate and relieve your stress response.*** *A rollicking laugh fires up and then cools down your stress response, and it can increase and then decrease your heart rate and blood pressure. The result? A good, relaxed feeling.*
3. ***Soothe tension.*** *Laughter can also stimulate circulation and aid muscle relaxation, both of which can help reduce some of the physical symptoms of stress.*

4. ***Improve your immune system.*** *Negative thoughts manifest into chemical reactions that can affect your body by bringing more stress into your system and decreasing your immunity. By contrast, positive thoughts can actually release neuropeptides that help fight stress and potentially more-serious illnesses.*
5. ***Relieve pain.*** *Laughter may ease pain by causing the body to produce its own natural painkillers.*
6. ***Increase personal satisfaction.*** *Laughter can also make it easier to cope with difficult situations. It also helps you connect with other people.*
7. ***Improve your mood.*** *Many people experience depression, sometimes due to chronic illnesses. Laughter can help lessen your depression and anxiety and may make you feel happier.*

An old Jewish proverb says, *"As soap is to the body, laughter is to the soul."* Laughter can cleanse us. A deep bout of laughter can often be the cheapest form of therapy.

Mark Twain, that master of satirical humor, once said, *"Power, money, persuasion, supplication, persecution—these can lift at a colossal humbug—push it a little—weaken it a little, century by century, but only laughter can blow it to rags and atoms at a blast. Against the assault of laughter, nothing can stand."*

"Laughter is the sun that drives misery from the human face," Victor Hugo.

The quotes and evidence that laughter is beneficial on many levels goes on and on. However, there is something even more important than a few moments spent laughing at a party or parked in front of your favorite sitcom and that is inner joy. Those people who have learned to laugh through and at anything have done so because they have learned the power of a **MERRY** heart, aka, a positive attitude.

Proverbs 15:15 says that a cheerful heart has a continual feast. Happiness is a foundation and joy is an expression of love. However, you have to choose joy. We all face things that bring us down. We all face disappointments. We can either wallow in them or find the light and focus on it.

It's hard to go form grief to joy, from despair to peace, so what we do is no matter where we find ourselves, we reach for a higher feeling. It doesn't have to be much higher, but the reaching lifts us up.

No storm lasts forever.
Regardless
Of how hard wind blows
Or thunder bellows
Regardless of how violently
Lighting rips clouds
Or rain pounds earth.
Every tempest whimpers.

Whimpers then surrenders.
To steadfast stars
Unaffected
Objective
Observers
Of temporary tantrums.
~darlene franklin campbell, 2015

LOOK UPWARD and INWARD

I remember an old saying I read in a discarded, discount book called *How to Stay on Top When the Bottom Falls Out* that changed my existence. I was seventeen, shy, alone and in over my head. Trust me when I tell you that my bottom had fallen out. Within three years my grandmother had died of a heart attack, my brother had been killed in an accident and my thirty-eight-year-old mom had suddenly passed away. My father was sinking into grief and depression. I was struggling with anorexia and thoughts of self-harm. I felt there was something innately WRONG with me and that somehow, I didn't deserve to live. I felt like I was never good enough and that people expected perfection I couldn't give them. To make a long story short, my young life was complicated.

All the trust-worthy adults in my life were gone and I was expected to be the adult.

I found that ragged paperback book in a box of junk someone gave us, and, in that book, there was a quote, *"Two men looked out of prison bars. One saw mud. The other saw stars."* The author went on to say that our perspective changes everything. He quoted another author saying, *"Your attitude determines your altitude."*

I made a decision that day. No matter how muddy it was, I was going to see stars. On cloudy evenings, I would remember that the stars were still there, just on the other side of the clouds.

A tornado may be blowing at the moment, but no storm lasts forever. The sun is always, ALWAYS going to shine again and the stars will return to the night sky. I decided that I would choose joy.

I have a saying that I sign my work emails with, "Happiness is a choice, not a set of circumstances." *(I think I made that one up, but most likely someone else said it first.)* I can't help but think that the secret to a happy life isn't in the things we have. It isn't in the grand experiences we can give ourselves or others. The secret to a happy life is found in taking the moment we are in and consciously being thankful for whatever positive thing presents itself. It might be as grand as dinner in a palace or as simple as a dandelion peeping through the crack in a sidewalk.

Corrie ten Boom told of a time when she was in a concentration camp and saw a dandelion poking its head through the cracks in the concrete. She rejoiced. Her sister, Betsie, rejoiced over fleas in their barracks because the fleas kept the guards out. Paul, a man who wrote much of the New Testament, said, "Rejoice always." One of the laws of the spiritual universe is to choose joy. Gratitude brings happiness and joy. Joy brings laughter and laughter brings healing.

The Way of Light and Love

Chapter Ten
Humility

Photo by Rachel A. Warmouth

"Whosoever therefore shall humble himself as this little child, the same is greatest in the kingdom of heaven. Matthew 18:4

"Only great humility and great love allow one to obtain the Great Power, Which is the same as the Power of Tao (the power of the Way)." Lao Tzu

"Happy are the humble: for theirs is the kingdom of heaven," Jesus from the Sermon on the Mount

Humility.

The very word grates on some people because they have a false concept of it. Apparently, some people think that humility and self-deprecation are one and the same and that to be humble you have to be a doormat. No. No. And NO. That is NOT the meaning of humility.

According to Merriam-Webster's humility is FREEDOM from pride or arrogance.

Wait a minute. Pride and arrogance are things from which we need to be freed?

Yes, in the sense that pride and arrogance (which is an extreme sense of self-importance and desire to be adored and admired by others) are the cultivation, preservation and exaltation of self-esteem and importance. Constantly, being a slave to "looking good," is definitely a type of bondage.

To obtain a sense of humility then is to obtain a type of freedom. What exactly IS that freedom?

It's the independence of not needing to prove yourself to anyone, to not need praise or approval. That doesn't mean that you don't appreciate it when it comes, merely that you don't need it or crave it and it's the freedom from having to look good (be approved of) in the eyes of others.

I think it was Ralph Waldo Emerson who said, **"A great man is always willing to be little."**

Here's an example. Once upon a time in ancient Israel, a teenager named David went out to the battlefield to take food and wine to his brothers who were in the army. He was just a scrawny kid, a shepherd, a nobody from nowhere. No one looked up to him or respected him. He had no claim to fame.

While being an errand boy to his brothers, a giant came out and made fun of the entire Israeli army. David was appalled and asked something like, "Who is this guy and why doesn't anyone stand up to him?"

His brothers were embarrassed by his naive presumption that somebody ought to put this terrifying threat in his place. David then said he'd go fight that giant and his brother's accused him of being arrogant! But nothing was further from the truth. Human approval meant so little to the boy that he was willing to lay his life on the line to do what he believed was the right thing to do.

People laughed at David. They ridiculed him. If there was any pride or arrogance in him at the moment, he would have backed down, but he didn't.

David cared more about being true to what he knew was right than about what society said or what anyone thought of him. Pride doesn't do that. Pride wants to look good and get accolades. Pride likes to have a little "worship" from others and craves approval and admiration.

David went out to face the most terrifying foe in his world, armed with the simplicity of a shepherd (seriously, the kid had a pouch full of rocks!). The enemy came at David with the best armor the world had to offer at that time. He was superior and he bragged about his superiority. David had only his simple faith, "I come to you in the name of the Lord," he said. There was no bragging about his own might or ability. But he was confident in the source of his strength.

David ran to the battlefield in humility, just doing what he needed to do where he was at. He had nothing to prove and nothing to lose (well, except his life). That is humility. He wasn't thinking about himself, but about his God and about his people.

If you have ever read the story then you already know that David slung his stone, which struck Goliath in the head and knocked him down. David ran over, picked up the giant's sword and beheaded him with his own weapon.

When the opposing army saw how a youngster had defeated a seasoned champion, they were terrified and fled the battlefield with the armies of Israel hot on their trail. If David had been engulfed in "pride" or concern over how he looked in the eyes of everybody else, the battle would never have been won.

It's worth noting that the person who demands that they be noticed, adored, and admired is arrogant, but so is the person who won't do things because they're worried that they might "look bad" in front of other people. That is still a type of pride. Arrogance often wears the disguise of politeness and nice-ness.

Being shy or reserved does not equate with humility. Doing everything within your power to keep from standing out does not equate with humility, either. For example, the person who gets on stage and sings his heart out, knowing that he may fall flat on his face or be laughed off stage, exhibits more humility than the musician who worries what others will say and keeps his music all to himself. The artist who never shares her work is more prideful than the one who allows herself to be vulnerable and shares it with the world in hopes of touching someone's life. It's not about whether we're center stage or not. It's about motivation. A closet narcissist is still a narcissist; they're simply better at disguising their pride in the garments of false humility.

Consider the following true story that I once witnessed.

I was in a group where a gentleman was asked to sing a song. The man stood up and protested, "Oh, I'm not very good at singing," he was digging in his pocket for his song as he spoke. "I'm just a poor man who does his best, and..." he was now making his way to the platform in the front of the room, "Y'all just listen to the words and not to why I sing them." He walked with his eyes toward the ground, showing us all that he was shy and humble.

Once on the platform, he dispelled other self-depreciating words to let us know what a humble person he was. Of course, people were encouraging him, telling him how great he was and pleading with him to continue with his song. They were nodding with softened and sympathetic expressions, but something bothered me about the entire episode. Then it hit me. This man was not humble at all. He was PROUD. That's right; he was proud of his own perceived piety! He was proud of his humility. He wanted everyone to know that he was humble and therefore, spiritual. I almost laughed.

Real humility doesn't need recognition or fanfare. So, what would have been the truly humble response? Easy. He would just gotten up, walked up front, said something like, "I hope you enjoy this song." Then he would have sung it and gone back to his seat. The most humble thing he could have said would have been thank you.

"True humility does not know that it is humble. If it did, it would be proud from the contemplation of so fine a virtue." – Martin Luther

Humility simply means that you are secure enough in who you are and in what you believe that you have nothing to prove to anybody, you don't feel the need to impress anybody, and you are able to use the God-given gifts or life-skills you've acquired to betterment of humanity without needing accolades or praise. This spiritual principle or law is expressed when Jesus said that the greatest among us was the one who willingly served others, not the one who demanded to be served. The greatest leader is the servant.

"...avoid putting yourself before others and you can become a leader among men. "- Lao Tzu

If you want others to find you interesting, show interest in them. If you want others to appreciate you, appreciate them. If you want to make a difference in the world, lay aside your concern over the way you appear, your need for approval and let the gifts within you come forth. An apple tree doesn't care what it looks like, it simply produces apples. It doesn't matter that some people may not like apples or that others may say the apples or the tree itself are ugly or disgusting or they may ridicule the tree. The truth is that fruit provides nourishment to wildlife and passersby and the tree itself provides shelter for many life-forms. Humility is simply bearing your fruit in this world and being what you were made to be without regards to praise or criticisms.

I close with a quote from Rick Warren, a California pastor, who said, "Humility is not thinking less of yourself. It is thinking of yourself less."

"God resists the proud but gives grace to the humble. Therefore, humble yourselves under the mighty hand of God, that he may exalt you in due time."

I Peter 5:5-6

Chapter Eleven
LETTING GO

"Which means more to you, you, or your renown?
Which brings more to you, you or what you own?
I say what you gain is more trouble than what you lose.
Love is the fruit of sacrifice.

> *Wealth is the fruit of generosity.*
> *A contented man is never disappointed.*
> *He knows when to stop and is preserved*
> *from peril,*
> *Only thus can you endure long."*
> Tao Te Ching verse

Lao Tzu's words speak to me. They probe my heart, asking me, "What is truly important to you?" When I really look at this, I realize that it's not anything "outside" of me that is most important to me. It's my connection to God, my consciousness, my inner peace and source of strength and joy.

Jesus asked, *"For what shall it profit a man, if he shall gain the whole world, and lose his own soul?"*

In his book *Change Your Thoughts, Change Your Life*, Wayne Dyer says, "Some people spend their entire lives seeking more of everything—possessions, money, recognition, award, friends, experiences, places to go, substances, food, etc." If you live by this philosophy, the search itself becomes your jailer.

Someone once told me, "The one who dies with the most experiences wins." At the time I nodded in agreement but later it came to me that I don't really believe that.

That philosophy doesn't ring true with the essence of who I am or as the Apostle Paul might have said, "That doesn't bear witness with my spirit."

Inner peace is the prize, not a string of extraordinary experiences. That doesn't mean that we can't have them, but they mean more when we don't HAVE to have them, when we don't NEED to have them. We are meant to have abundant life but when we learn to be content with the food on our tables, clothes on our back and roof over our heads, then everything else we get is just joy on top of joy.

Lao Tzu advises that what we acquire is more trouble than what we lose. Some people seek love but the second it turns to exerting control, it ceases to be love and becomes a power struggle. Love is never about power and control.

If we want to fix our relationships, then we need to work on ourselves instead of demanding others to change in order to fit into our schema of how things should be. When we do that, we are saying that there is something lacking in our lives and unless everyone else lines up with what we think we need, we can't be happy.

I realize in reading this passage in the Tao Te Ching today that the number one relationship in my life is between me and God, the source of my eternal existence. When I'm in alignment with the Spirit of God, then all my other relationships will fall into place as an extension of me being aligned with pure love. I'll love myself right and I'll love everyone else, too.

I like how Dyer puts it, "Go there first, before any other considerations, and you'll automatically discontinue demanding more of anything else."

Release attachments whether those attachments be to things, to an outcome or the way you want other people to think, feel and act.

There is freedom and peace that come from letting go.

"Practice not doing...When action is pure and selfless, everything settles into its own perfect place."
Tao Te Ching verse 4

Let go and let God. Realize that you don't have the power to control outcomes or reactions. Make your requests known to God and then let it go. Stop trying to "fix" everyone or make things happen, allow the dust to settle. Follow impulses from the Holy Spirit (you'll know them because they are always the way that causes you to feel the most inner peace), but don't do anything because you are being urged by people or seemingly threatening circumstances. Let the Source of All that is untangle the knots for you and watch how beautifully everything works out.

Chapter Twelve

GOING WITHIN

"Be still and know that I Am God." Psalm 6:10

Psalm 18:9 says, "He brought me forth into a spacious

place because He delighted in me." I need not strive or fight to obtain but rather live my life in faith, which is powered by the never-ending energy, spirit of love, God.

Lao Tzu says in verse five of the Tao Te Ching, "Hold onto the center. Man was made to sit quietly and find the truth within." In other words, "Be still and know that I AM God.

> "Just sit there right now
>
> Don't do a thing.
>
> Just rest.
>
> For your separation from God,
>
> From Love—
>
> Is the hardest work
>
> In this world."
>
> Hafiz

Once there was a man named Elijah who was so lined up with God that he knew things were going to happen before they happened, and he knew secrets that military leaders uttered in their private meetings. He saw extraordinary events that would be called miracles these days but there came a day when he felt down so he went to a cave to hide from a wicked woman.

He felt disconnected from God and sought to hear God in a tornado, but he didn't hear. There was too much commotion. He thought to hear God in a roaring fire, but again, there was too much distraction. He thought to hear God in an earthquake, but it was too loud and disturbing. It wasn't until he was alone in a quiet cave that he heard the voice of God. That's where he was sensitive enough to feel the spiritual impulses of his connection to this Creator.

In my own life I have found that I must retreat to places and moments of solitude in order to find my center and regain my balance in life.

I find my strength in quietness,
in waiting, observing, listening
to the voice of the One Great Spirit
as He speaks through wind in grass,
through cicadas in locust trees,
through falling yellow leaves of walnut trees
who find ending of summer too hot
and decide to shed their clothing.
He speaks to me through the salamander
black and yellow spotted, darting under mud
through algae floating in tiny green triads
and pears lying beneath their mother
through apples
crashing branches
flaunting their scent.
When I am invisible to men
inaudible to women
He still speaks to me and something leaps
within...
there is no greater sound.

Chapter Thirteen
Mind Your Own Business

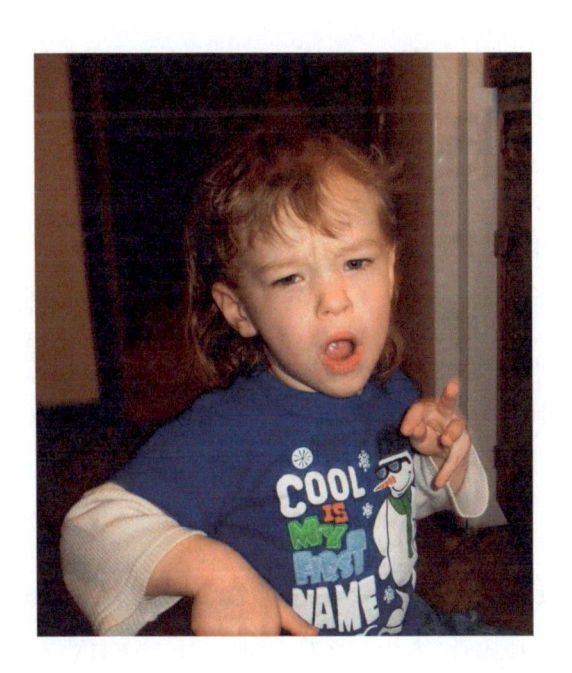

Kindergarten.

"Art Teacher," Bobby calls out, "Jimmy just hit me and said my picture is ugly."

"Jimmy, why did you hit Bobby?" I ask.

"Because" Jimmy says, "he's not coloring the sky blue. The sky is supposed to be blue. I told him to color his sky blue and he won't listen."

"So, you got mad?" I say.

"Yes."

"And you hit him to make him do what you wanted him to do?"

"No, it wasn't like that. He's not doing it RIGHT. The sky is *supposed* to be blue."

"So, Bobby is coloring his picture of his world differently than you think the world is supposed to look?" I say, "and you don't like the way he sees the world because it doesn't match the way you see it, so, you got mad at him and tried to make him do it the way you think it needs to be done. You hurt Bobby because you wanted him to make his world your way? Is that what happened?"

"Ugh," Jimmy says, "Yes, I got mad because he ain't doing right. And he won't listen to me when I try to tell him the right way to do it."

"And how is that hurting you?" I ask.

"But it's supposed to be blue!" Jimmy is clearly upset that anyone could see the sky as green, black, and purple instead of blue.

"And how is that hurting you?" I ask again.

"But...skies are blue."

"Your sky is blue," I say. "Bobby's is multicolored. What if you color your world your way and Bobby colors his world and you don't try to force Bobby's world to look just like yours? Then you will both have a better day."

"I want you to make him do it right," Jimmy says sullenly.

"Do you want to be right or happy?" I ask.

Jimmy and Bobby both look at me, confusion etched across their little faces.

I explain. "I'm not going to force Bobby to color his sky the way you want it to be. However, if you insist on being right, and hitting Bobby because he made a choice that's different than yours, then you are going to find yourself in a very unhappy position, say losing some of your behavior dollars, or you can accept that Bobby is different than you and that it's okay for other people to see the world differently, mind your own business, color your own sky and have a peaceful, happy day. The choice is yours. So, do you want to be right or be happy?"

Jimmy thinks hard for a moment. Letting go of the need to be right is tough. Then he says, "I'd rather be happy."

Bobby pipes up, "Me, too. I like to be happy." He proceeds to draw a purple sun in the sky.

Jimmy visibly cringes, but he chooses to be happy, at least for now. He hasn't seen Sophia's flying unicorn fish yet.

....

Jimmy and Bobby aren't my real students, but the scenario is real, daily.

I've been teaching for thirty-one years now and not one day goes by, rarely one hour goes by, in which some student isn't trying to force someone else to see things his or her way.

In this scenario, Jimmy's teacher is trying to let him in on a secret. It's the secret of peace. If we want peace in our lives, then we must stop trying to control the actions of others. No wonder Jesus said, "Blessed are the peacemakers for they shall be called the children of God."

That doesn't mean we go around settling arguments but that we facilitate inner peace. Outer peace without inner peace is impossible. The secret to having outer peace in the world is more people with inner peace!

As adults, we are not so different than Jimmy, concerned about what someone else is doing. Perhaps, it would be good if we could learn the lesson Jimmy's teacher is trying to teach him. We don't need to control others and the only actions we are ultimately responsible for are our own.

Ironically, we can see the tiniest faults in the behaviors of others yet neglect to see similar things in ourselves. Jesus once responded to some critics by saying they had the ability to see a speck of dust in someone else's eyes but couldn't see the giant beam sticking out of their own.

If I had a quarter for every time a child has come up to me and reported on the affairs of others in hopes that I would "punish" the other child, I would be as rich as Elon Musk!

It seems to start early, this need to control others, even when those actions have nothing to do with us. Kids will often say things like, **"Make them let me play** with their toy." Or **"Make them play** with me." Translation: "Do what I want YOU to do and MAKE THEM behave the way I want them to behave."

Sadly, this desire to control and punish others often doesn't end when childhood ends. It just graduates and grows bigger and instead of making someone give up their toy or play with them, the controllers want to dictate how others should live their lives. They want to invade neighboring countries, take over their resources and control their populations.

How much pain and suffering in the world would be alleviated if world leaders didn't try to make other countries conform to their wishes? If they didn't invade and seek control? What if everyone in the world were truly empathic?

When Jesus was born, the angels spoke to shepherds proclaiming peace on earth, but of course, the world hasn't been at "peace" since that time, but in the biblical sense, peace doesn't mean the absence of war. It means inner tranquility, staying calm regardless of what others are doing or saying. In other words, inner peace is only found when we let go of the need to control others.

You can't have internal peace so long as you're trying to control the actions of others. And just as Jimmy isn't justified in dictating how Bobby colors or one child isn't justified in forcing others to play, we are never justified in wanting to control the feelings and thoughts of others.

It's far too common and too easy to focus on the negative aspects of others, to talk bad about them and try to make them behave the way we want them to, but it's a losing battle and in the end, we accomplish nothing but destroying our own peace of mind and happiness. I once heard a young minister named Randy (who knows? Maybe he is reading this right now!) say, "You can't legislate morality." He was right. Kindness, goodness, empathy, joy, love.... those things must come from the inside out and be voluntary. If you force people into morality, it's not real and sooner or later the sleeping demons of self-righteousness, greed and power will awaken.

Peter, an early follower of Jesus, wrote, *"Do not repay injury for or insult with insult. On the contrary, repay injury with kindness, because to this you were invited so that you may obtain adulation. For whoever would take pleasure in, long for, and enjoy life (both physical and spiritual, present, and future) and experience good days must restrain his language from injurious and their lips from treacherous (deceitful and harmful) speech. They must cease from doing injury and do good; they must seek peace and pursue it."*

Likewise, Paul the apostle, once told a group of Thessalonians who were in The Way to aspire to live quiet and peaceful lives, to mind their own business and work with their own hands.

A passage from Psalms keeps going through my head:

> 46:10 He says, "Be still, and know that I am God;
> I will be exalted among the nations,
> I will be exalted in the earth."

The words "be still" there denote a "letting go" or "falling into." In other words, as Elsa says in Frozen, "Let it Go!" The word "know" means to recognize, get it, or understand.

So, we could put it in the modern vernacular, "Let it go! Relax, and recognize..." What are we recognizing? We are recognizing that I Am God. Which God? The I AM. And what are we recognizing? The fact that I Am is God! And whatever you need I Am is. Nothing is impossible with I Am God. Nothing.

Peace comes when we let go and relax in the knowledge that the Almighty Source of all that is or has been or ever will be is in control. Peace comes when we realize that a person's life-worth doesn't consist of our possessions, or what color we paint our skies.

Chapter Fourteen

Cheerful Givers

Photo by Rachel A. Warmouth

IN THE BOOK OF ACTS, Paul quoted Jesus as having said that it is more blessed to give than receive but how can this be? The word "blessed" here was originally "makarios," which means to be fortunate. So, Paul and Jesus were saying the giver is more fortunate than the receiver. But doesn't it seem like that the more you have, the more "blessed" you are?

GIVERS ARE HAPPIER IN LIFE

A 2002 survey of 30,000 Americans **showed that those who gave to charity, whether financially or in the form of volunteer work,** were far happier than non-givers. It is almost like the more you give away cheerfully, the more you have to give away. The cheerful aspect is a **HUGE** component in all of this. If a person gives out of a sense of obligation and resentment, no happiness comes to them from it, and they are robbed of their "blessing" or status of being fortunate.

WHEN WE ARE CHEERFUL, WE ARE ALSO COURAGEOUS

Giving is an act of courage and courage is an act of faith. Jesus told his disciples, "Be of good CHEER." The word cheer here literally translates into ancient Greek as COURAGE. So, every time we choose to be cheerful, we demonstrate an act of courage.

The great speaker, Wayne Dyer, said that one of the secrets to having contentment in life was to want more for others than you want for yourself, to wish good on them more than you wish it upon yourself. He said that if you want peace in your life, then wish for and pray for others to have peace. If you have an addiction and want to be free of it, wish for, pray for and hope for others to be free from addiction. If you wish to be financially blessed, want others to be even more so. Living this way requires courage and brings joy.

That seems so contradictory to the "me first" mentality of greed. But if the whole world, or even 20% of the world, lived by those rules then there would be far less pain in the world, far less need. Instead of struggling to survive, people could explore and learn and there is no telling what the human mind and spirit could accomplish. It would be like the thousand years spoken of by Isaiah the Prophet where people beat their swords into plowshares and instead of killing each other, they feed each other. Instead of stealing from each other, they give to each other. Sounds like a good place to live to me. I believe greed is born of fear and giving is born of courage.

CHEEFUL GIVING IS A DEMONSTRATION OF LOVE

One could say that giving is how I Am demonstrates love toward us. Jesus, in speaking to Nicodemus said, "For God so loved the world that He gave...." He gave.

When the Israelites were wandering in the desert God gave them water. God gave them food. They got fearful, greedy, and tried to hoard it, so it spoiled on them, but nevertheless, he GAVE. Giving is the nature of God. The true nature of the Great I Am. Giving is an extension of love and according to John, God is Love. (1 John 4:8)

GIVING DEMONSTRATES CONFIDENCE IN GOD'S ABILITIES

Our willingness to give demonstrates our view of I Am's ability to provide for us. If we hoard and are fearful of tomorrow, of not having enough, we communicate that we doubt there are enough "riches in glory" to provide for our needs. Being fearful of giving demonstrates a lack of confidence in God's approval of and love of us, in LOVE's identity. In demonstrate doubt in I Am's, Jehovah Jireh's, the Almighty Source's, Klongliwiha, The Great Spirit's, He Who Never Dies,' ability to provide what we need when we need it. Jesus addressed this by talking about the birds of the air and the lilies of the fields. That doesn't mean we should never have a bank account or a savings plan, only that we are not so stingy that we can't "share" out of our abundance.

The Tao Te Ching talks about how the wise person, the person of virtue, gives out of his or her abundance or excess. If I have two coats, I can afford to give one away without being fearful of life without that extra coat because I might "need it someday." The key to being fortunate, in all areas of life, according to Jesus, Mother Teresa, Gandhi, Lao Tzu, Apostle Paul, Saint John, Saint Francis, Wayne Dyer, the Dali Lama and every other spiritually attuned deity, person or teacher, is to cast fortune on others. They can't ALL be wrong!

GIVING IS CONTAGIOUS

In the movie, *Pay it Forward*, a little boy produces the idea of doing good deeds for others with "pay back" being "paying forward." I give to you, and you don't pay me back, you give to someone else. I do good to you, and you do good for someone else.

So many people give but secretly, subconsciously, keep score and hidden contracts with the thought somewhere in the back of their minds, "I've done this for him (or her) now he will do things my way." That's not giving. That's bartering. I've heard so many people say, "I can't believe he'd do that after ALL I'VE DONE FOR HIM." Or "Can you believe she said that to me after how nice I'VE BEEN TO HER?" These are hidden contracts. If you give expecting performance, you've already missed the boat. Giving should be for the soul purpose of making another's life a little better. If you don't WANT to give for the pure joy of doing it, then you're better off not to give at all. Paul said to give cheerfully, not begrudgingly. Expect nothing in return and receive everything from a Source far greater than you can imagine.

SOMETHINGS ARE SO EASY TO GIVE

A smile, the touch of a hand, a word of encouragement, a note, a card, a smiley face, a cup of coffee, a piece of fruit, a moment of laughter, a joke. It merely takes an act of courage, of getting outside ourselves, and being a cheerful giver.

Random Thoughts

I think God's plans are better than what you have planned for yourself.

I read, "A man's heart deviseth his way: but the Lord directeth his steps." Proverbs 16:9 KJV

I ask myself, "What does that really mean?" I turn to the Strong's Concordance for an answer and learn:

A person's feelings, will and intellect may fabricate, plot, or contrive his or her life course, road, or path, but God, the Self-Existent, Eternal One, sets up his or her pace, prepares, establishes, readies, stabilizes, provides—directs that person's path.

Jesus told us to take no thought about tomorrow. In other words, stop trying to solve tomorrow's problems while it's still today. Do what the Spirit of God is telling you to do today and watch how tomorrow will work out as it should.

Now, this moment, faith is the substance of things hoped for and the evidence of things not yet seen in the physical realm. All things, ALL things work together for those who love God and are guided by his plans. That's me. I love God and aspire to be guided by the Holy Spirit. Yes, that's me.

Chapter Fifteen
Peacemakers

"Blessed are the peacemakers for they shall be called the children of God." Matthew 5:9

WHAT'S A PEACEMAKER?

We often think of a peacemaker as someone who settles disputes, but in this context the word peace indicates something more. It comes from a Greek word, Eirene (irah-nay) which means to set at one again in quietness and rest (Strong's Concordance). So, what was Jesus really saying? In John 14:27, he told his disciples that he gave them peace but not like the secular image of peace. He went on to say, "Let not your hearts be troubled." Sounds to me like he's talking about inner peace.

INNER PEACE COMES FROM INSIDE—THAT'S WHY IT'S CALLED "INNER" PEACE

According to the Tao Te Ching, "In order to maintain calm (peace), one has to feel oneself as an integral part of the Absolute. Then one does not develop false ego-centric desires." In other words, The Absolute, the Almighty, is not an entity that exists outside of us but is an ever-present part of us. We can't obtain what Paul calls "peace from God," by keeping laws, following rules, buying things, controlling others, etc. We must recognize that only by believing that we are who God says we are (and it's always good. People assign "badness" to us, not God. Our Creator loves us, believes in us, values us, and appreciates us.) There are those who are out of alignment with who they really are, who do horrible, ungodly things to others and to themselves because they don't know who and what they really are; the spirit within them seems dormant, but it's there, just waiting to be awakened, to be born again.

STOP TRYING TO "FIX" EVERYTHING

I love what Wayne Dyer said about peace and I believe he is onto something, *"Peace is the result of retraining the mind to process life as it is, rather than as you think it should be."* Or as the Apostle Paul said, *"Be content with such things as you have." (Hebrews 13:1)*

I remember reading one time, *"Two men looked out of prison bars. One saw mud. The other saw stars."* They were in the same situation, but one was at peace and hopeful while the other was depressed and in turmoil.

PEACE RELINQUISHES THE NEED FOR POWER AND CONTROL

Paul referred to God as the "God of peace." God is love. Love casts out fear. Fear has torment so there is no peace in fear. All motivations ultimately come down to one of two motivations: Love or Fear. Greed comes from fear and greed, the love of power and the fear of not having it, is at the core of every inhumane act on the planet.

Therefore, any act done in fear or out of its off-spring, greed, is not an act of peace, not an act of love, therefore, it's not an act of God, because remember God doesn't have love. God IS love. (See I John).

Did you ever think that maybe if each person in the world found inner peace that there would also be outer peace? Outer turmoil is a sign of inner turmoil.

Again, I quote from the Tao Te Ching, *"Being satisfied with little, you can gain much. Seeking much, you will go astray. The wise heed this percept. If it could only be so with all people! The wise trust not only their physical eyes, thus they can see clearly. The wise do not think that they alone are right, thus they know the truth. They do not seek glory, yet people respect them. They do not seek power, yet people follow them. They do not fight against anyone; thus no one can vanquish them. They do not feel pity for themselves; thus, they can develop successfully. Only those who do not seek to be ahead of others are capable of living in harmony with everyone."*

DON'T STOP DANCING

Joseph Campbell, the great student of mythology and world religions, had studied many cultures and came to a conclusion that no matter where people were from, if they failed to be true to that inner guidance system, that voice inside them urging them to follow their "calling," at some point they would feel regret from not doing it. I recall specifically, a story of a ballerina who gave up a promising career in dancing, because her husband was threatened by her success. She gave up her dancing, her passion, her gifting, her call in life. Many times, in her life she lamented giving up the dancing, always telling her children how she once was an excellent ballerina. Years later, after the husband was long gone and her kids were grandparents, she was alone in a nursing home, in her nineties with dementia. She couldn't remember anyone's name, but she remembered how to dance, so she would get up beside her bed, do ballet and bask in the applause of her imagined audience. She finally found her inner peace. The point of this story is two-fold, no matter how much we "love" someone, it is never required that you hide your light under a bushel to appease their insecurities. That will not bring you peace. We cannot forsake our life's calling because someone else is afraid to follow theirs.

LET PEACE GUIDE YOUR STEPS

In Romans 14:19, Paul encouraged those who be "in the Way" to follow after the things which make for peace and in another place, he urged the believers in the Way to let the peace of God guide them, rule in their hearts. He encouraged them in Ephesians to have their "feet shod" with the preparation of the good news of peace. This peace which comes from I Am passes all mental acknowledgment and understanding. It's a spirit thing.

Random Thoughts:

The Lord is MY shepherd. Our relationship is personal. I exist because his Love is the Energy that fills me with Light and animates this body and mind. This Love, Light and Energy are the Spirit of God, and the Spirit gives life. Where the Spirit of God is, there is freedom. Love is the core of who he is. This love empowers me to shine.

Lord, that goes back to the term Yahweh and that means I Am; I Am is a present experience. I Am is my shepherd. The good shepherd gives his life for his sheep. The good shepherd says, "I Am come that you might have life and life more abundantly." I am in a covenant with I AM who daily loads me with benefits. Therefore, everything is always working out for me. How can it not? If I AM is for me and in me? What power on earth can be greater? If I AM LOVE is flowing through me, what have I to fear in this world? Perfect LOVE casts out all fear. Wow. Just wow.

Chapter Sixteen

ASK

⁵And when thou prayest, thou shalt not be as the hypocrites are: for they love to pray standing in the synagogues and in the corners of the streets, that they may be seen of men. Verily I say unto you, They have their reward.⁶ But thou, when thou prayest, enter into thy closet, and when thou hast shut thy door, pray to thy Father which is in secret; and thy Father which seeth in secret shall reward thee openly.⁷ But when ye pray, use not vain repetitions, as the heathen do: for they think that they shall be heard

for their much speaking.⁸ Be not ye therefore like unto them: for your Father knoweth what things ye have need of, before ye ask him.⁹ After this manner therefore pray ye: Our Father which art in heaven, Hallowed be thy name.¹⁰ Thy kingdom come, Thy will be done in earth, as it is in heaven.¹¹ Give us this day our daily bread.¹² And forgive us our debts, as we forgive our debtors.¹³ And lead us not into temptation, but deliver us from evil: For thine is the kingdom, and the power, and the glory, forever. Amen.¹⁴ For if ye forgive men their trespasses, your heavenly Father will also forgive you:¹⁵ But if ye forgive not men their trespasses, neither will your Father forgive your trespasses. ~Matthew 6:5-15

WHAT IS PRAYER ANYWAY?

Simply put, most of the time when the word is used in the New Testament it simply means to ask, petition, or entreat. Sometime the word "pray" makes me think of books I've read or movies I've watched where people spoke an older version of English and said such things as, "I pray ye, Sir, canst thou spare me a penny?" In other words, "I'm asking, could you give me a penny?" Our modern word, pray, comes from an Old French term which comes from Latin, but the word used in the New Testament comes from Greek and while the English and French variations imply begging, the Greek means to ask and sometimes it means to worship which means to honor, adore, and appreciate. It is my understanding that praying means to ask with an appreciative, expectant attitude, not a begging attitude. That means you don't have to crawl up the steps of an elaborate church on your hands and knees, weeping, flogging yourself and begging God to have mercy on you, a dirty, rotten sinner. Prayer simply means to respectfully ask with appreciation and gratitude as if the answer is already given.

OUR FATHER– The Greek word Jesus used here "pat-ayr" translates as "parent or father parent." In Jewish tradition at that time the role of a father was to protect, to provide, and to love as is evidenced in stories such as the one where Joseph's father lamented the perceived loss of his son so deeply that he never got over it. It was expected that a father not only claim his children but actively love them in words and in actions. Wow. That means God actively loves us in words and in actions.

Notice that Jesus didn't just say, "*my Father.*" He said OUR Father, OUR parent, OUR source, OUR provider." Why is this so important? Because Jesus wanted us to know that his father and OUR father are the same Father, so by his saying OUR, he let us each know that we can confidently say MY. So, OUR Creator, is also our parent, because like an author who could give life to his/her characters, Creator loves us, appreciates us, cherishes us and is truly a Father to us.

WHICH ART IN HEAVEN

The Greek word for Heaven here, according to *Strong's Exhaustive Concordance*, is Ouranos which implies rising, above, a habitation, happiness, eternity—i.e., a higher plane or a place of eternal happiness. Old timers around here used to call it Glory. I remember an old song, "Just over in the Glory Land." Heaven is as good a term as any, but we could say, "Our Father, you exist in a higher realm, outside the confinements of this "book of life," and when the covers are closed, you still exist. You can intervene anywhere and at any point. There are no limitations in your reality."

HALLOWED BE THY NAME—

sacred, pure, and blameless is your onoma (Greek), which means character, authority. In other words, you (Father) are sacred, pure, blameless. There is no ill-will toward me, toward any of us. We are, I am, loved without measure and due to nothing I (nor anyone else) have or have not done.

THY KINGDOM COME. THY WILL BE DONE ON EARTH AS IT IS IN HEAVEN.

Let your kingdom come in me. Let your peace, which is incomprehensible to those who don't believe you exist in a reality beyond all that we can imagine, guide my heart, my every step. I want to do things in the way that you say is best for me. I want your directions to be sovereign in my life. I want to walk the perfect pathway that you have laid out for me and trust that you know where all the pieces to my life's puzzles go and that you know how to help me write the next chapter in my life story. I want to see my journey as you see it. I want your help in authoring my story, because you are the author and editor of all that I believe, and I know that you know what is best for me.

GIVE US OUR DAILY BREAD

There is no limit in the higher reality. There is no lack. There is only abundance in every area. Whatever I need, it's already there. So, I petition you, "Give me what I need today," and I thank you for it. My heart is full of excitement that you will do exceedingly, abundantly above all that I ask or think according to the power, the same power that created the universe, formed the world, that works within me. I will not worry over tomorrow because you are already there.

AND FORGIVE US OUR DEBTS, AS WE FORGIVE OUR DEBTORS

Debt implies owing. Somewhere Paul said that we owe no one anything except love. Forgiveness implies not holding a wrong done to you against someone. Jesus never said to pray to "Forgive and forget," only forgive. So, I pray, "Overlook my faults and I overlook the faults of others." And I also pray, "Let me see through spirit eyes and look at others the way you look at them."

AND LEAD US NOT INTO TEMPTATION

Help me not to get distracted from the right path. Guide me away from things, people and circumstances that would divert me and keep me from the values that you have placed inside me: peace, joy, love, hope, faith, creativity, honest relationships, kindness, gratefulness, appreciation, mercy, gentleness, health, satisfaction, and abundance in every area of my life. Keep my eyes focused on my purpose and my feet on the path that is right and best for my life. Help me to constantly be aware of the bigger picture.

BUT DELIVER US FROM EVIL

Set me free and steer me clear of everything in my life that brings degeneracy to me, that would hurt me, influence me to go in a direction that is not best for me, steals my wealth, hurts my family, works to stunt my spiritual growth, harms my physical body, emotional state, or mind, from anything that would hinder me, bring calamity upon me, grieve me, or divert me from the best path for my life. *(Evil in this passage indicated illness, calamity, degeneracy—hurt; also, I Chronicles 4:10 Jabez prayed something similar.)*

FOR THINE IS THE KINGDOM— AND THE POWER—AND THE GLORY—FOREVER—AMEN,

Your way is the best way, the only true way, and the only enduring way. Your reality is the only one that *is* reality to me, and all that exits is because of your will, your intent, your imagination, your purpose. Let me have joy in this world and in the world to come. I thank you for eternity. Let these all these things come to be.

And after having searched the meanings of each word in Jesus example, I feel inspired and thankful, so I talk to my Father from the depths of my spirit and I say,

"Thank you, God, for everything, for always working things out for my good and for your glory, so that people see your hand upon my life and know that you are good, so that people see the good works your love compels me to and stand in awe of your goodness. Nothing that is made or has been made can exist without your love energy. I give my every problem to your all-knowing awareness. You know all the answers to all the issues I encounter in this life. There is nothing that exists which is beyond your ability to untangle and resolve. Thank you for solving the problems I see right in front of me and the ones that I haven't yet foreseen. I need not worry anymore. I need not lose sleep, fret, or struggle to find answers. In the moment I need them, they will be there. I trust you, God. I trust The Way; the wisdom of Jesus and I know that as I see him, I will be as he is in this world. I choose to build my life upon His words, upon The Eternal Way of Light and Love.

I hold nothing against anyone. I do not cast blame, wish punishment or shame upon anyone. I know that you will work all things out and so I put my every concern over my loved ones and relationships in your hands.

I thank you that even if I step off the best lifepath you have for me that if I call out to you for help, you will set my feet aright. You will not leave me nor forsake me. You are not capable of doing so because you live within me. Your light fills my vessel and I know you are my Father, my Source, the essence of my existence.

Your Way is Light, and your Way is Love and your Way is the only true Way, your Light is the only true Light and by your Will this world exists and because I am from you, your child, I exist, too. Forever. I belong to the Kingdom of Light and Love. Amen.

Freedom

An ongoing state that is absent of restraint, necessity, coercion, constraint in choice or action, liberation from the dominating influence of others.

Chapter Seventeen

Stories

Photo by Marilyn Boyd

I am an author and as such, I view life through the eyes of a creator, a creator of realities, plots, and characters. What you are about to read is an understanding so big that it is difficult to even put it into words, and although I got a glimpse of it years ago, it wasn't until I sat down to write this blog post that it became so profound as to expand my understanding beyond anything I have previously known.

WHY DO WE LOVE STORIES?

THE ADVENTURES OF...the mystery of.... the tales of.... You name it and there is a story about it. So, why do we love stories? Why do we create stories?

It's because we love adventure. We love discovery. We love excitement (albeit all of us love it on different levels). We love to dream and to imagine, to wonder. That's why we're drawn to what we don't know, what we haven't experienced.

Imagine that you came into life already knowing the entire storyline and there was nothing for you to discover or wonder about or uncover. What if there were no adventures or mysteries? Nothing would excite you because you'd already know everything. It'd be like living in a rerun.

Helen Keller once said that life is a grand adventure or nothing at all. She was blind and deaf, yet she could hear and see on a level that many never reach. So, the joy of writing a story is in watching the characters evolve, discover, and explore.

What if these characters were more than figments of the author's imagination? What if they were sentient? What if I could give them life and the ability to make their own choices and to draft their own stories? Now THAT would be interesting!

THE OMNIPOTENT AUTHOR

If the characters in one of my novels could talk to you, they would speak only from the perspective of their world, which is held within the confines of the manuscript that I, the omnipotent creator of their reality, have written for them. They would have no idea that they are simply extensions of my imagination, unless of course, I gave them the ability to know me and the freedom to choose whether to trust my judgement as to how to best complete their stories.

If I, as an author, could give sentience to my characters, I would love them as if they were my children and there would be nothing, I wouldn't do to help them love their own stories, to enjoy their grand adventure through their book of life. So, why would I do this? For my good pleasure or well, just because I wanted to create something THAT amazing. But what would be the best way to make them aware of my existence and give them the chance to interact with me?

A UNIQUE CHARACTER

I could just create them with complete understanding and knowledge, but then they would miss out on the experience of knowing what it is like to begin a story as flat characters and then to become aware of the fact that they are more than just computer bites or ink on paper, or figments in a dream, lifeless with no control over what happens to them. They would miss out on the experience of "waking up" and realizing that they are literally sent into the story to play there and discover much like children are when going to a new playground. They would miss out on the discovery of learning that they are co-creators with me and that I am giving them whatever they ask for in their stories. They would miss out on knowing the joy that comes with "waking up," and discovering who they really are.

I could drop hints that might help them wake up. Maybe, throughout the unfolding of the plot, especially in the early chapters, I would interject myself into the story so that some of the characters got glimpses of me. These characters might try to tell the others what they had seen, heard, and understood, but they'd be limited to the language of the story. So, the things they said would often be misunderstood.

Of course, some of them would form crazy ideas about me, based on a partial picture, because after all, they are sentient. They might make up all kinds of rules about who gets to receive their special knowledge and the rules might become more important than the adventure of the story itself. They might spend their entire time in the story, making up rules and trying to tell other people how the story is supposed to unfold.

Some of them would try to force the other characters to act the way they wanted them to, threaten, guilt, manipulate and control them into doing so. They could even take to writing each other out of the plot (killing one another off). I could intervene, but that takes away the free will that I already chose to give them.

ONE OF THEIR OWN

I suppose the best way to communicate who I really am and that I really want to see them create and have fun doing it would be to write a unique and special kind of character, a representative of myself! My special character, because he or she knows exactly who I am and what I really want would do things that defied the laws that other characters had written into the book, because those laws were written with limited understanding.

This character to whom I would give complete knowledge and memory of being with me and a part of me before coming into the world of the story would be a creation the same as all the others and would live in the same confinements of the book.

However, this character would understand that he or she and all the other characters existed outside the book within me before they came into the story. This character would know that they came into existence because I wanted to create them, give them life, and let them experience the joy of waking up. Even more than that, he or she would know that I not only wanted to give them life, but the ability to choose what kind of life they would live.

THE AUTHOR WANTS TO HELP THE CHARACTERS

OF COURSE, the role of this character would be to tell the others about me and how I was gifting each of them with the power to create their own stories. If they choose to create with their limited understanding of what is true by refusing to believe that I exist and thinking that what's in the book is all that there is; then they are on their own, and their stories might not be what they really want, because they can't see what's up ahead and how all the pieces of the plot fit together, but if they ask me for guidance, I will intervene and steer them away from consequences that they want to avoid. I will gladly use my literary expertise and help them write a fantastic life story.

I would have my special character share the message with a few of them and then I'd take him or her out of the book, because they will spread the message in the following chapters. And if they understood what I was telling them through my special character, they would discover that they, too, were extensions of me and that I had given them the ability, the power, to change the plot of their stories and shape them in ways that they really wanted.

Once awakened to what they are truly capable of, they would be so happy and joyful in the discovery that they would want to share it with others. There would be some, of course, who weren't awake but were astonished by those who were, so they would make up more rules and laws and ways of doing things to teach others how to be aware.

THE ILLUSION OF DEATH AND CONTROL

This special character coming into the story with full knowledge would already know how the story was going to play out. He or she might know that many wouldn't believe the message that I was giving them the power to create themselves. They might be so bent on staying within the confines of the book that they create all kinds of havoc, even to the point of killing off the special character that I sent into the story, but me, being the omnipotent author, could resurrect that special character and re-insert him or her into the story with not only the message that I exist but proof that I can do anything, because in relation to their reality, I have no limits. I, the author, could resurrect the dead at will, because I would want them to understand through this that "death" is an illusion. It is not an ending. It is only an exit from the story.

Death is the beginning of a new kind of existence, one with limitless understanding and because there is limitless understanding, there is no sadness, no fear, no hate.

So if one of my characters were to ask me for assistance, no matter how jumbled their story has become, no matter how out of alignment with what they really want for themselves it has gotten, no matter how much of it they've let other characters write, if they ask me to help them straighten it out, I will gladly intervene, and it would be so much fun for me to talk to my characters and have them talk to me. What could be more delightful to a creator than to have a living creation to whom you have given sentience, communicate and co-create with you?!

The only thing that could even come close to that feeling on earth is doing things with your kids and seeing delight and discovery on their faces. In that way, I, the original creator of the story, would be a parent to all my characters and I would be their source and the answer to every dilemma they might encounter, but I would honor the free-will that I had given them and not force them to do anything. However, if they ask me to help them write the plot, because I see the whole book from cover to cover and I know the best course of action for them, then yes, I will rework the plot on their behalf and work things out for them.

Chapter Eighteen
Hope

"For I know the plans I have for you," declares the Lord, "plans to prosper you and not to harm you, plans to give you hope and a future."
Jeremiah 29:11

Martin Luther King Jr. once said that it's only in the darkness that we can see the stars. So, the darker the night, the more obvious a star. A literal translation of that for those not so metaphorically inclined is that it's only in a troubled time, a dire situation, the face of discouragement, that we really notice hope. If all things are going smoothly then we don't have to exercise hope so much. But hope is that which breaks through our darkness. As Desmond Tutu once said, "Hope is being able to see that there is light despite all of the darkness."

Once I went to Mammoth Cave. The tour guide turned out the lights. The darkness was the darkest dark I had ever seen. Then she turned on her flashlight and everywhere that single light source touched was lit. No matter how dark a place is, just one small light, so long as it shines, makes a difference in whether you walk with sure footing or you fall into a crevice. Never underestimate the power of a light, a ray of hope, no matter how small it may seem.

Over the past two years, we've been bombarded with images of darkness (metaphorically speaking). The news has been filled with disease, plagues, floods, fires, earthquakes, tornadoes, hurricanes, war, threats of more wars, possibly biological warfare, riots, political unrest, upheaval in every realm imaginable; mayhem, death, destruction, despair, and discouragement, but whenever I go out at night, the first thing I notice is the stars, the light.

If it is raining or cloudy, then I notice every porch light or every glimmer of the moon that lightens the clouds. Light is energy and it always finds a way to get through, even if it's just through cracks or around the edges of a shade.

The Way of Light and Love

One sliver of light drives away the darkest dark. So, I'd like to focus on a few slivers of light, of hope.

Hope is free. It is no respecter of persons. Hope doesn't care where you come from or what shade of fleshly vehicle you're driving through your life on earth. Hope is an equal opportunity encourager. It is not bound to geographic regions, not stopped by prison walls, not squelched by floods, or burned away by fires nor buried in landslides.

Hope, the earnest expectation of goodness on its way; it is unstoppable so long as we refuse to let go of it. Even in death, if we leave this world in hope, refusing to let go of it, we leave a light for others. I believe we are eternal, spiritual beings. You can't kill a spirit. You can't kill an eternal being. You can only destroy the body that houses it. Hope is the flower pushing its way up through a crack in life's sidewalk. Hope, like air, like water, like light, like life, like eternal love—finds a way.

We can each be a source of hope to others and since in we are all connected, each time we offer hope to others, we receive it back to ourselves as well.

How can we be a source of hope? Here's a few examples:

*A man on my street just mowed his sick neighbor's yard–no charge.

He didn't ask what political party the neighbor belonged to or whether or not he was vaccinated. He was a source of hope, not judgement.

*A woman just bought groceries and dropped them off at a sick person's house.

She didn't say, "Pay me back for my trouble." She was a source of hope, not racking up an account on a covert contract.

*A nurse in a COVID unit just helped a patient charge his Ipad so he could FaceTime his family.

Even though it wasn't the reason she was in his room. She went above and beyond her pay. Her kindness was a ray of sunshine, a beam of hope.

*An immigrant walking his dog past an emergency room door, stopped to cheer up a woman whose husband was inside with a possible pulmonary ambulism. She waited outside, not allowed in the hospital, and uninformed of her husband's condition, nervous, anxious, sacred and in need of hope.

He didn't care that she was from a different cultural background. He was an example of human kindness, a ray of hope.

*A boss just gave an employee extra time off because her father was ill, and she wanted to be with him.

She didn't complain about someone else having to work extra hours. She showed compassion and empathy, a ray of hope.

*A lady in the checkout line just told the boy behind the counter that she appreciated his work ethic and thanked him for showing up to do a job that keeps the country running.

She didn't complain about having to wait a little longer in line than she usually likes to wait. She offered encouragement, another ray of hope.

*A lady in North Carolina just said a prayer for a young man from her hometown who is being flown to Afghanistan.

It didn't matter that he isn't her own son. She showed compassion-hope.

*A church group of volunteers just set up a free food day in their parking lot to help feed their community.

They didn't ask for proof of citizenship, vaccination, or income, tribal ID cards or proof of blood quantum. They just fed people and offered them hope.

*A young Black girl just celebrated her 13th birthday with her White mother and grandmother, Black grandmother and boyfriend and White cousins who are like brothers to her.

Nobody even mentioned skin tones. They just laughed, loved, and played together because they're family and they all gave her words of a hopeful future, many birthdays to come.

*A teacher just spend half the summer setting up her classroom for the students that are coming back. She prayed over every chair and the child that would sit in each seat. She planned her bulletin boards and hung posters and curtains and prepared record books and on and on and on...even ordered hermit crabs and fish, because she loves her kids and wants them to have the best experience possible at school.

*She was only given $200 in funding to prepare her classroom. She spent $500.00 and school hasn't even started. So, most of it came from her own purse. She can only get tax credit on $200 out of pocket expense. She will spend a lot more before the year is out. But she does it in hope that her kids will learn and know that they are loved. For **some** kids, a teacher is the only rare of love and hope they see.*

The good is all around us. The light is shining. Perhaps today you can think of someone who has given you hope or some sign of hope that came to you when all seemed to be sinking around you. And maybe, you are also a ray of hope to someone else.

We need each other. The darkness would have us divided over issues and policies, but hope reminds us that we are all great spiritual beings and this life on earth is better if we see each other that way. Not one of us can actually see what's inside another person's heart and not one of us knows what miracles a single act of kindness can set in motion because that act has restored hope or perhaps awakened it for the first time in someone's life.

Chapter Nineteen
The Way of Light

*"In him was life; and the life was the light of men.
And the light shineth in darkness; and the darkness comprehended it not."*
John 1:4-5

"You are the light of the world...let your light so shine that men may see your good works and glorify your Father which is in heaven." ~Jesus, Matthew 5:14 NKJV

The God energy that created this world is Love and when you are filled with that energy you are light. So many people have no clue that they are vessels of an eternal light, that they are eternal beings. Some are so captured by the ideologies of this world that they literally fear coming into contact with the Light and actively oppose anything that threatens their concept of reality.

They may go so far as to label the Light as evil and confuse The Way as the oppressor when in truth it is the only thing that can give them real freedom in this world. They mistakenly believe that happiness is found outside themselves, in the possession of things, political power, fame, accolades and rewards, in controlling others, in relationships, etc., but it is only found in waking up to their connection to the Source of all that is.

They oppose, often loudly and violently, the very thing that could give them freedom and peace, choosing the ways of this temporal existence rather than the eternal ways of God. They have no idea of who they really are. They are lost to themselves, even when they have status and acclaim and the goods of this world, they are actually blind, poor, naked, and foolish.

However, when one is touched by the energy of Love they will awaken to the Light within and no longer be a slave to fear.

No matter what you face, remember that you are not alone. Right now, many people are hurting, and many people are afraid but there is a LOVE in this universe that supersedes everything, and that LOVE is a living entity that gives life to all things and connects us.

That LOVE is an ALMIGHTY SPIRIT, and that spirit resides in all who reach out and believe. That is the same SPIRIT that Jesus talked about, that same SPIRIT can restore us, heal us, and remind us that we, too, are

SPIRIT.

The real me is not the body I live in. My body is just a vehicle with which to travel in the mortal realm. My gender, my culture, my ethnicity, my epidermal melanin concentration, my height, weight, age nor any other facet of my flesh and blood existence on this earth, is the real me.

The spirit of me is the real me and I pray that I see past the flesh of others and see them as an extension of the Great Spirit. The real me is an eternal great spiritual being and the laws of the Spiritual Universe override the laws of the physical universe.

What can separate us from the LOVE of God, that same LOVE that resides in Jesus Christ? The same LOVE (Spirit) that performed miracles? Nothing. Right now, if you are hurting, if your loved one is sick, if you are facing financial difficulties, if you are hungry, if you are homeless, if you are facing a disease yourself, if you are being bullied, if you are being threatened, if you feel you have to perform to be lovable or that your beauty makes you worthy, if you are feeling worthless or guilty over something you did or didn't do, accept my "spiritual" hug and know this...you are loved. You are accepted. You are valuable beyond all words to describe, and you are a beautiful spiritual being.

Don't let the lies of this world darken you to the truth of who you are, of what you are. Believe that you are an extension of Almighty Love because you are. The Great Spirit of Love holds nothing against you...nothing. We are enough because of who we are. We just have to know who we are so we can believe it to be true.

Our lives emanate from the great light which is the source and beginning of all life in this world. Another word for that light within us is Spirit, Inner Man, Inner Being.

We are vessels which light inhabits, but most people don't know what kind of beings they really are. They don't know that they are actually an energy being on a temporary journey through a physical environment. When you realize this, you can say, "Oh, death where is thy sting? Oh, grave where is thy victory?" *(I Corinthians 15:55 KJV)*

Let you lights shine. When your light shines you exude peace. You are filled with joy. You are forgiving, and patient. You abhor violence and extend mercy. You deliver grace and speak with gentleness. You exert restraint and act with kindness. You are content with what you have, not comparing yourself to others to make them seem less so that you seem more and not slyly fishing for compliments. Wow, I think Paul called these—fruits of the Spirit. Evidence of those who walk in The Way.

[22] But the fruit of the Spirit is love, joy, peace, forbearance, kindness, goodness, faithfulness, [23] gentleness and self-control." (Galatians 5:22 KJV)

Chapter Twenty

The Way of Love

Photo by Bonnie Franklin

In my newest work in progress, the main character, Addie, has spent her life believing she was insignificant until a chance encounter with someone from a dimension where the only law is love, turns her world upside down.

What if we realized that there really is one great law in the universe that supersedes all others, and that law is the law of Love? I promise you that when you come to this knowledge and you experience the energy of this Love firsthand, it will open up a whole new realm of existence for you and it will give you the power to not only see reality but to alter it.

I've noticed a lot of fear around me lately, fear of COVID, fear of the government, fear of the vaccine, fear of control, fear of hunger, fear of losing jobs, fear of...well, just fear of fear. But what exactly is fear?

Perhaps fear is what we experience when we take our eyes off what God's path for our lives, even if it's momentary and put them on what we don't want. We don't have to stay there. We can move past it. Perhaps the ultimate fear is the fear of death but what if we realize that the only way out of this life is dying and that sooner or later, we're all going to do that anyway. It's the only way out of this realm unless a miracle transformation happens and whisks us all out of here.

Fear keeps us in bondage, keeps us from being the people we were created to be. I've heard it said that we aren't humans having a spiritual experience from time to time. We are SPIRITS having a human experience for a short span in the expanse of forever. What happens to us in this life is brief. Even if we lived to be 150 years old, our time in this mortal realm is still short. Truthfully, nature abhors a vacuum and fear is what fills the void when love leaves the room. Fear is the absence of love. The moment you let love back in the door, fear is gone. It dissipates like water vapor in a desert.

I am convinced with everything inside me that there is basically nothing else in life as important as understanding who we are, what we are and where we came from and to grasp those basic spiritual concepts of what it means to be alive, we must realize that the ONLY things that matter are fear and love.

Ultimately, LOVE is the only thing that matters. The only one. Also, please realize that when I speak of love, I speak of something far, far greater than "romance." Romance was invented to sell novels, candy, and Valentine's Day cards. It's not even necessary to procreate. I suppose it's just fun but then it leads to this feeling of possession which stems from fear of losing someone which is stems from a lack of love. Jealousy is NOT a sign of love. Jealousy is a sign of the erroneous belief that you have power and control over another human being and that you somehow think you possess them. Love never possesses. It always liberates. Fear possesses and creates bondage. The old saying, "If you love something, set it free," is true.

So, again I say, there are only two motivations for every act on earth: fear and love. Whatever is not done because of love is done because of fear and vice versa. What so many of us don't get is that we must FIRST LOVE OURSELVES. That means we must accept ourselves as valuable and of great eternal worth. Jesus didn't say "Love your neighbor but treat yourself like a doormat." No. He said, "Love your neighbor AS yourself." In other words, you also MUST LOVE YOURSELF! If we don't first love ourselves, we have no hope of loving others and we will spend our lives doing things out of guilt, out of fear that someone will get angry with us and out of fear of not being accepted. Yep, there's that fear again.

So, love yourself like your life depends on it because it does. It's both simple and hard. We think we fear is a thing, but it isn't. It's only what exists when there is no love. We create fear by removing love.

The Apostle John tells us that "God IS love. And everyone that is born of God is born of love and he that does not love does not know God." Notice that he doesn't say, "God has love." No! He says, "God IS love." You can literally substitute the word "is" with an = sign! I make this point to say that we all come from God, so we all come from love. We are born knowing that we are loved. We come from love and when we die, we return to love. It's while we are here that we forget who we are and where we came from. I am a LOVE CHILD (I'm not talking about my physical body. That's only my earth vehicle, kind of like a rental car), because I came from LOVE, and that love is GOD.

It is important to remember that we are loved and to love ourselves because when you don't love yourself you believe everyone else is better and that their message is better than yours. How often do we make ourselves small so others can be big? We dim our lights so that others can feel brighter because we've bought into the lie that some of us are less important than others. We're not. We say yes when we mean no because it's easier to disappoint ourselves than others. We are facets of God, all of us. If we don't love ourselves, we don't allow ourselves to express who we are. We are not allowing a facet of God to express itself through us. Our purpose for being here is to love. You don't have the right not to love ourselves. We must love ourselves. What is love? Love is sincere acceptance and appreciation of who someone really is and that includes yourself.

Every day, all around us, people are hurting. We are all connected and if you are constantly needy and in search of validation and approval, if you have a big hole in your life that no amount of praise or validation can't fill, you bring others down. But if you love yourself and are joyful, happy, and fulfilled, then others want to be around you. People who are sick can sense your energy, by the way, and the last thing a sick person needs is negativity around them. Negativity is when you have this black hole that just sucks other people's energy to try to make yourself feel better, but it never works. The only way to fill that hole is to realize that you are loved by your creator, that you are a part of this marvelous universe, that you have worth.

Loving yourself is a form of being selfless to the people around you. Wherever you go, you bring yourself with you. Your presence is what changes your surroundings. If you bring a needy self, that is what you put out into the world. You are doing a service to the world when you love yourself. This is what shining your light means. I leave off today with this thought, "Love yourself as you love your neighbor." Accept yourself as work of the Almighty, as an extension of pure love. We don't have love. We are love and unless we live knowing that we are made of love, come from love and are love, we are living a lie. Love is the only truth, and it is this truth that sets us free to be lights in this world. Be the light. Love yourself.

Remember.

Love doesn't force people to bend to its will, doesn't manipulate them into conforming, guilt them into acting, intimidate them into surrender, interrogate them into sorrow or dismiss them into despair. Love simply accepts people as they are and asks nothing in return. Love has no strings attached and no covert contracts.

ABOUT THE AUTHOR

Darlene Franklin-Campbell, author, artist, and teacher is from South-Central Kentucky. She makes her home between the Green and Cumberland Rivers in the foothills of Appalachia. She is a member of the Mysterium Society, The Elizabeth Maddox Roberts Poetry Society, The Sheltowee Artisans Guild, The Adair County Arts Council, New Life for the Nations Church, The Adair County Genealogical Society, and the New River Band of the Catawba Nation. Darlene is an avid student of the Bible and the Tao Te Ching. She also works to preserve Native American languages, art, history, and culture. She holds an M.A. in Literacy in Education from Lindsey Wilson College and is the author of six novels including *Looking for Pork Chop McQuade, Touched* and the award-winning, *I Listened, Momma. The Way of Light and Love* is her first non-fiction work. To contact Darlene

you can visit her website at https://www.dardet.com or follow her on Facebook at https://www.facebook.com/therealdardet/
And on Instagram at dardetart

"This is the WAY, walk ye in it."
Isaiah 30:21

Darlene Franklin-Campbell

A prayer very similar to this one, prayed over the course of seven months has changed my life. Maybe it will bless yours as well.

Heavenly Father,
I know that I am an eternal spirit. I will always be. I know that my life comes from you. You are my Source and inside of me, there is a place of freedom, of divine confidence and centeredness, a calm that is secure. Here, in this spirit realm, The Way, are the answers to all my "problems," which are only illusions for I am divinely connected to you. Even now those answers are on their way into this natural realm. I don't have to worry, fret or struggle. I don't have to plot, plan or scheme, only trust that when the time comes, the solutions will be there. I give all of my hangups, faults and problems to you. I lay my burdens down and will carry them no more. I know that all things work together for the good of those who Love you and that's me. I love you. I need only believe.

I thank you for providing my needs, I thank you for not blaming, shaming, or abandoning me when I falter and err from the path. I choose to do the same to others. I will not let roots of anger, bitterness or resentment take hold in my life, leading me to spew negativity into this world. I will abhor that which is violent and harmful to myself and others and I will shine as a light for the Love which is you fills my life and lights my way.

Today, I choose to be a host to divine LOVE which is the source of all that exists and the only thing that is everlasting.
I thank you that the same power which raised Jesus, the promised Messiah, from the dead, lives in me and gives life to my mortal body. I know that nothing is impossible so long as I believe. Therefore, I believe. With my whole heart, soul and mind, I believe and I love you.
Amen

Darlene Franklin-Campbell